themes for early years

C000177990

SCHOLASTIC

People who help us

Fully revised with CD-ROM

Licence for CD-ROM

IMPORTANT – PERMITTED USE AND WARNINGS – READ CAREFULLY BEFORE INSTALLING

Includes Adobe Reader

Adobe, the Adobe logo, and Reader are either registered trademarks or trademarks of Adobe Systems Incorporated in the United States and/or other countries.

To enable the running of the videos on the CD-ROM please download the latest version of Apple QuickTime from http://www.apple.com/quicktime/download/win.html

For all technical support queries, please phone Scholastic Customer Services on 0845 603 9091.

To use the activities on the CD included with this book, you will need the following:
- PC with CD and 128 Mb RAM with Microsoft Windows 98SE or higher
- Mac G3 with CD and 128 Mb RAM with System 8.6 or later (Mac OSX classic model only)
- Facilities for printing and sound
- SVGA screen displaying at least 64K colours at a screen size of 800 × 600 pixels.

Jenni Tavener

themes for early years

Credits

Text © 2007 Jenni Tavener
© 2007 Scholastic Ltd

Published by Scholastic Ltd, Villiers House,
Clarendon Avenue, Leamington Spa,
Warwickshire CV32 5PR

Printed by Bell & Bain Ltd, Glasgow

2 3 4 5 6 7 8 9 0   8 9 0 1 2 3 4 5 6

British Library Cataloguing-in-Publication
Data A catalogue record for this book is
available from the British Library.

ISBN 0-439-94498-8
ISBN 978-0439-94498-4

Visit our website at www.scholastic.co.uk

CD-ROM developed in association with Footmark
Media Ltd.

All songs and rhymes performed by Sally Scott and
Simon Anderson.

On-screen activities developed in association with
Ugly Studios © 2007, Ugly Studios

Author
Jenni Tavener

Editor
Jane Bishop

Assistant Editor
Rachel Mackinnon

Series Designers
Joy Monkhouse, Anna Oliwa,
Andrea Lewis and Catherine Mason

Designers
Allison Parry, Sonia Bagley, Erik Ivens,
Anna Oliwa and Geraldine Reidy

Illustrations
Gaynor Berry

Cover artwork
Maria Maddox

Acknowledgements

Extracts from *Themes for Early Years: People who help us* by Anne Farr and Janet Morris (1997, Scholastic):
Ann Bryant for the use of 'The wheelie bin song' by Ann Bryant © 1997, Ann Bryant. **Debbie Campbell**
for the use of 'The driver of our school bus' by Debbie Campbell © 1997, Debbie Campbell. **Jillian Harker**
for the use of 'The Fireman' by Jillian Harker © 1997, Jillian Harker. **Carole Henderson Begg** for the use of
'Friends and neighbours' by Carole Henderson Begg © 1997, Carole Henderson Begg. **Hazel Hobbs** for the
use of 'Guess who?' by Hazel Hobbs © 1997, Hazel Hobbs. **Wes Magee** for the use of 'Crossing the Road' and
'Postie, Postie' by Wes Magee © 1997, Wes Magee. **Trevor Millum** for the use of 'Whose hat is that?' text by
Trevor Millum © 1997, Trevor Millum. **Tony Mitton** for the use of 'Guess Who?' by Tony Mitton © 1997, Tony
Mitton. **David Moses** for the use of 'Meet my dentist (what a nice man)' by David Moses © 1997, David Moses.
Judith Nicholls for the use of 'The Dentist' and 'Haircut' by Judith Nicholls © 1997, Judith Nicholls. **Gillian
Parker** for the use of 'Whose hat is that?' music by Gillian Parker © 1997, Gillian Parker. **Jan Pollard** for the
use of 'The Bin Men' by Jan Pollard © 1997, Jan Pollard. **John Rice** for the use of 'Farmer' by John Rice ©
1997, John Rice.
Sally Scott for the use of 'People who helped us' by Sally Scott © 2007, Sally Scott (previously
unpublished). **Brenda Williams** for the use of 'Shopping on the internet', 'Here comes the caretaker' and
'Visiting the nurse' by Brenda Williams © 2007, Brenda Williams (previously unpublished).
Qualifications and Curriculum Authority for the use of extracts from QCA/DfEE document Curriculum
guidance for the foundation stage © 2000 Qualifications and Curriculum Authority.

Every effort has been made to trace copyright holders and the publishers apologise for any omissions.

Contents

themes for early years

CD-ROM
- All songs sung with musical accompaniment
- All songs music-only version
- All rhymes spoken
- 18 photocopiable pages
- Ten full-colour photographs
- Five on-screen activities
- Three film clips

Introduction

Using themes in early years

Themes can help practitioners to provide a relevant and interesting learning environment. The theme of 'People who help us', for example, encompasses many aspects of the world in which we live and can be used to help children develop a greater awareness of their local environment and the variety of different communities within it.

Themes can also help to foster positive attitudes by providing children with a main focus for gathering and sharing information or making collections for example, sharing the CD-ROM, seeking books, collecting pictures or photographs and bringing in relevant artefacts from home. All of these encourage children to work, play, talk, listen and respond to each other appropriately.

How to use this book

This book focuses on the theme of 'People who help us' and offers a variety of activities and support material which link directly to selected Early Learning Goals and Stepping Stones as identified in the *Curriculum guidance for the foundation stage* (QCA). The Planner on page 7 shows how each activity fits in with the six Areas of Learning.

Each chapter within this book deals with a different aspect of the theme. The first chapter focuses on people who help at home and encourages the children to consider how this help affects their home life. The second chapter focuses on the early years setting and provides opportunities for the children to find out about the important role of key workers, volunteers and visitors. In Chapter three, activities focus on people who help to keep us healthy, for example, doctors, nurses and dentists. The children are encouraged to explore these professions and to investigate how they help us and why.

Chapter four looks at people who help to keep us safe, for example, firefighters, police and lifeboat crew. The children are given the opportunity to find out about people who are brave during their every day work or perform

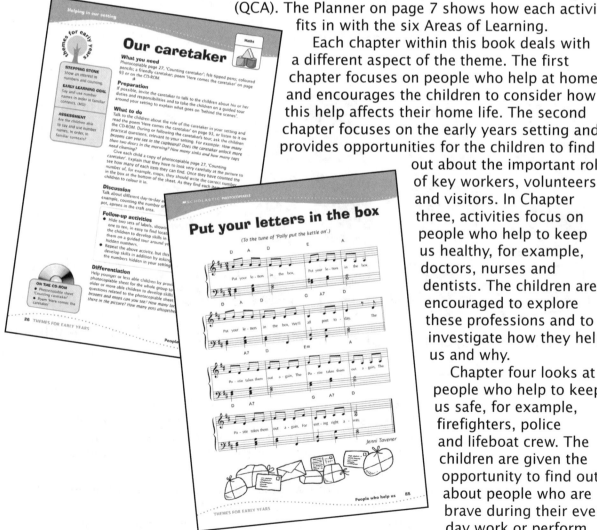

specific acts of bravery to help others. Chapter five takes a look at people who help to bring us food and information and the children are encouraged to explore how this help affects our lives on a daily basis. Chapter six can be used to help the children gain a greater awareness of people who are dedicated to helping the community or the local environment.

A display section offers ideas that can be used to help develop the children's interest and enthusiasm for the theme via practical activities such as making games, creating gifts, taking photographs and constructing models.

The resources section provides a variety of songs, poems and action rhymes based on 'People who help us', all of which can also be found on the CD-ROM.

What's on the CD-ROM?

The CD-ROM with this book contains ten photographs, three film clips and five on-screen activities, in addition to audio versions of all the songs and poems and printable versions of the photocopiable pages in this book.

The ten photographs include: a lifeguard, a dentist, a nurse, a roadside rescue patrol, a window cleaner, a hairdresser, a vet, a postperson, a crossing patrol person, and school cooks.

The three film clips show intriguing footage of people who help us. Two of the clips are of brave people who rescue others on a daily basis: a helicopter crew winching someone to safety and firefighters in action. The third is a more common sight of refuse collectors who help us all on a regular basis.

There are five on-screen activities relevant to the theme of 'People who help us'. The five activities are: 'Let's shop!', where children are encouraged to count fruit; 'Healthy lunch box', children have to place healthy items into lunch box; 'Emergency service vehicles', a jigsaw activity, where the children have to match the two halves of the emergency vehicles; 'Fairytale shoe shop' children have to drag and drop shoes to put them on the correct characters and 'Post the letters' where children take on the role of a postperson to deliver letters and parcels to the correct house.

The children will also be able to select audio versions of the songs, poems and action rhymes detailed in the resources section and print off copies of the photocopiable pages.

Can you deliver the post to the right houses?

Planner

Use this guide to link the activity ideas into your planning for the six Areas of Learning.

Communication, Language and Literacy

Mathematical Development

Personal, Social and Emotional Development

People who help us

Knowledge and Understanding of the World

Creative Development

Physical Development

themes for early years

Assessment

Gaining evidence of the children's skills, knowledge and progress is best achieved by using 'on-going' assessment, noted down when spotted and gathered at a later date. The child or children being assessed should be in familiar surroundings and provided with activities or challenges that they enjoy. A range of 'on-going' assessment procedures can be used at different times, depending on the children and the setting, for example, observations from a distance, listening to the children, joining in with play sessions and tracking children's achievements.

Observations from a distance

These can help practitioners to assess how a child or group of children interact without adult intervention and can also help practitioners to become aware of children who find it hard to join in with others or, conversely, to discover children who tend to take the lead. From these observations, your team can organise situations or activities to cater for the needs of children who lack confidence or enjoy the limelight. Role play activities provide ideal opportunities for this type of assessment, for example, 'Doctors and surgeons' on page 34 and 'The police' on page 43.

Talking, listening and joining in

To gain an insight into what the children know, remember, understand and recall, talk and listen to them during and after activities. The information that you gather can inform differentiation tasks for individuals who might require support or extension activities. Use the Discussion sections in this book as a guide to relevant questions, comments or queries. Talking and listening to the children as they view, describe and discuss the photographs and film clips on the CD-ROM can also provide an ideal opportunity for assessing language, vocabulary and comprehension.

Actively taking part in the children's games or joining in with creative tasks can provide an insight into the children's problem-solving abilities and decision-making skills. Opportunities for joining in with games and creative activities in this book, include, 'We help our friends' on page 12 and 'Removal workers' on page 16. Joining in with the children as they tackle the on-screen activities and challenges on the CD-ROM will also offer a wealth of opportunities for assessment.

Tracking achievements

Used in conjunction with other on-going procedures this involves viewing samples of the children's work, with parents or carers, to provide an indication of how individuals have progressed over a period of time. Materials gathered in this way can also provide an up-to-date and informative insight into each child's manual dexterity and hand-control. Useful activities for this include 'Gift tag' on page 15 which can illustrate handwriting skills and 'On Monday I ate' page 25 which can show drawing skills.

At home

Children's first knowledge of people helping is at home and many children love to play at 'helping' by washing the dishes, going shopping and cleaning the car.

themes for early years

Our parents and carers

Art and craft

What you need
A3 coloured card; black paper (slightly smaller than A4); felt-tipped pens; variety of collage materials cut into narrow strips (for example, paper, tissue, lace, fabric and ribbon); glue.

What to do
Talk to the children about the many ways in which their parents and carers help them during their everyday life. Invite the children to make a special card for their parents or their carers with a surprise 'Thank you' message on the front.

Give each child a sheet of A3 coloured card to fold in half. Help the children to write 'Thank you' in large letters on the front using colourful felt-tipped pens. Next, provide each child with a sheet of black paper and several colourful collage strips. Encourage the children to twist, curl, overlap and glue the strips on to the black paper to create a decorative, random pattern. When dry, help the children to place the design on the front of the folded card and to glue it in position along the top edge to create a decorative flap that lifts up to reveal the words 'Thank you'. Help the children to write a personal message inside their card.

Discussion
Talk to the children about the importance of saying 'Thank you' when somebody has helped them.

Follow-up activities
- Help the children to write their address on an envelope and to buy a stamp to post the 'Thank you' cards to their parent or carer.
- Encourage the children to design and make a card with a special message hidden behind a flap or picture.
- Create an 'Our helpers' display, see page 75.
- Help the children to complete the on-screen activity 'Let's shop!'.

Differentiation
Help younger or less able children to copy or trace the words 'Thank you'. Encourage older or more able children to help cut the collage materials into narrow strips.

STEPPING STONE
Try to capture experiences and responses with music, dance, paint and other materials or words.

EARLY LEARNING GOAL
Express and communicate their ideas, thoughts and feelings by using a widening range of materials, suitable tools, imaginative and role play, movement, designing and making, and a variety of songs and musical instruments. (CD)

ASSESSMENT
Are the children able to express and communicate their ideas, thoughts and feelings during discussion and shared activities?

ON THE CD-ROM
- On-screen activity 'Let's shop!'

Art and craft

themes for early years

We help at home

STEPPING STONE
Describe experiences and past actions, using a widening range of materials.

EARLY LEARNING GOAL
Respond in a variety of ways to what they see, hear, smell, touch and feel. (CD)

ASSESSMENT
Can the children recall experiences and past actions, using the collection of materials to prompt their memory?

What you need
Photocopiable page 11, 'Who helps?'; display board at the children's height; colourful backing paper; thick wool or ribbon; sticky tape; glue; paints; paintbrushes; paper; examples of household items used for cleaning such as a tea towel, duster, dustpan and brush.

Preparation
Cover a display board with colourful backing paper and mount a large label in the centre that says 'We help at home'.

What to do
Show the children some examples of household items used for cleaning and talk to the children about the different ways that they help their parents or carers at home, for example, dusting, making their bed, putting toys away or helping with the washing-up.

Provide the children with some colourful paints and encourage each child to paint a picture showing one of the ways in which they help at home. Position the paintings on the display board around the central label. Link the paintings to the label using lengths of ribbon to create a 'web' display. Help each child to write a caption to display near to their painting, for example, 'Jimmy helps to wash up', 'Ash helps to make his bed' or 'Sita helps to pick up her toys'.

Show the children photocopiable page 11, 'Who helps?' and ask them to draw the people who help with each of the four tasks in their home. If the children help with any of the jobs, encourage them to draw a picture of themselves. Help the children to write the name of each helper under the drawing.

Discussion
Gather the children into a group and look at each child's sheet. Ask the children to talk about who the helpers are and what they do.

Follow-up activities
● Encourage the children to join in with role play situations in the home corner based on helping our families.
● Invite the children to create a simple 'Thank you' card for someone who helps them at home. For example: 'To Grandad, thank you for helping me to ride my bike'.
● Share the poem 'There was an old woman' on page 92. Use this as stimulus for creating 'A shoe full of helpers!' display, see page 77.

ON THE CD-ROM
● Photocopiable sheet 'Who helps?'
● Poem 'There was an old woman'

Differentiation
Scribe the words in the captions for younger or less able children. Ask older or more able children to have a go at reading the captions on the display.

People who help us

Who helps?

Outdoor environment

themes for early years

We help our friends

What you need
Safe open space; one large cardboard box per team; one basket with two handles per team; one non-breakable toy (for example, balls, teddy bears or beanbags) for each pair of children.

Preparation
Divide the children into teams. Place the large cardboard boxes on the floor in a line to represent toy-boxes. Place one toy for each pair of children in the toy-boxes. Help the children in each team to form a line approximately 15 to 20 paces away from their toy-box.

What to do
To play the game, the first pair of children in each team should help one another to hold a basket as they run to their toy-box. They should pick one toy from the box and place it into the basket before running back to their team. If they drop the toy, they must stop to pick it up and replace it in the basket.

The first pair of children then passes the basket containing the toy to the next pair of children. The second pair of children in each team should take the basket to the toy-box to collect a second toy. This pair of children should then run back to their team, making sure both of the toys remain in the basket. Continue playing in this way so that each pair of children has a turn. The winners are the first team to remove all the toys from the toy-box, or just play for fun.

Discussion
Talk to the children about how they help their friends and how their friends help them at home, in your setting or during outside clubs.

Follow-up activities
● Adapt the game by asking the children to help one another carry the toys in their arms instead of using a basket.
● Provide the children with a wide range of collage materials, paints or colourful pens and ask them to create a picture about the game.
● Sing the song 'Friends and neighbours' on page 79, or listen to it on the CD-ROM.

Differentiation
Ask younger or less able children to carry only one toy at a time. Provide older children with soft balls to carry. This will require the children to carry the basket very evenly between them to avoid the balls bouncing out.

ON THE CD-ROM
● Song 'Friends and neighbours'

People who help us

Mark-making

We help ourselves!

STEPPING STONE
Relate and make attachments to members of their group.

EARLY LEARNING GOAL
Form good relationships with adults and peers. (PSED)

ASSESSMENT
Are the children willing to participate fully in group activities by joining in with others and forming good relationships with adults and peers?

What you need
Area where the children can sit comfortably; circles of card or thick paper (approximately 30cm in diameter); paints; paintbrushes; paper; thread.

Preparation
Paint or draw a simple smiley face on to both sides of two card discs.

What to do
Sit in a circle together and give two children a smiley face card each. Encourage the children to join in with the song 'Your smile is big and happy' to the tune 'The sun has got his hat on':

> Your smile is big and happy,
> Hip, hip, hip, hooray.
> Your smile is big and happy,
> And you're sharing it today.

Ask the two children holding the smiley faces to pass them around the circle as everyone sings. When the singing stops, ask the two children holding the smiley face cards to stand up and swap places, greeting one another with a smile, a wave or by shaking hands. Continue until all of the children have had a turn at swapping places with another child.

Next, talk with the children about how a smile can help us to feel happy by asking them to compare a smile with other expressions. Ask questions such as: *Does a cross look make you feel happy? Do you feel happy when you see a sad face? How do you feel if someone frowns at you?*

Provide the children with paints and paintbrushes and several circles of card or thick paper. Encourage them to paint a smiley face on both sides of the circle. When dry, hang the faces at varying heights to create a cluster of mobiles to illustrate the song.

Discussion
Talk with the children about songs and poems that help them feel happy.

Follow-up activity
● Give each child a small disc of card. Invite them to decorate it with a smiley face on one side and a sad face on the other side. Help them to attach a long, narrow strip of card to their disc to create a happy/sad face mask for role play.

Differentiation
Help younger children to keep up the momentum of passing the two smiley face discs around the circle as everyone sings. Encourage older or more able children to paint a smiley self-portrait for the mobile.

Stories and rhymes

themes for early years

Our grandparents

What you need
Comfortable place for the children to sit; drawing and writing materials; photocopiable page 15, 'Gift tag'.

What to do
Help the children to adapt a short and simple poem to suit a special person in their lives. Begin by encouraging the children to join in humming the tune to the first verse of the traditional song 'Old Macdonald had a farm'. Then introduce some new words to the familiar tune, for example:

> *My lovely* (person's name, for example, *Nanny, Grandpa, Auntie*),
> *Lives near me/lives away/lives with me,*
> *E–I–E–I–O!*
> *He/She is so kind and he/she loves me,*
> *E–I–E–I–O!*

Support each child in inserting the person's name in the first line, selecting the most appropriate words for the second line and including the words 'he' or 'she' in the fourth line, for example:

> *My lovely Granny, lives near me,*
> *E–I–E–I–O!*
> *She is so kind and she loves me,*
> *E–I–E–I–O!*
> *My lovely Uncle, lives away,*
> *E–I–E–I–O!*
> *He is so kind and he loves me,*
> *E–I–E–I–O!*

Help the children to write their adapted poem on photocopiable page 15, 'Gift tag' to give to their special person or to attach to a gift.

Discussion
Talk to the children about their special person and encourage them to explain why they are so special.

Follow-up activities
● Encourage the children to paint a picture about their poem.
● Write the poems in bold letters and display them on the wall with pictures of the children's special people. You could encorporate this into the 'Mark of appreciation!' display, see page 78.

Differentiation
Scribe the adapted poem onto the gift tag for younger or less able children to illustrate with pictures or patterns. Encourage older or more able children to write their poem in their favourite colours.

Gift tag

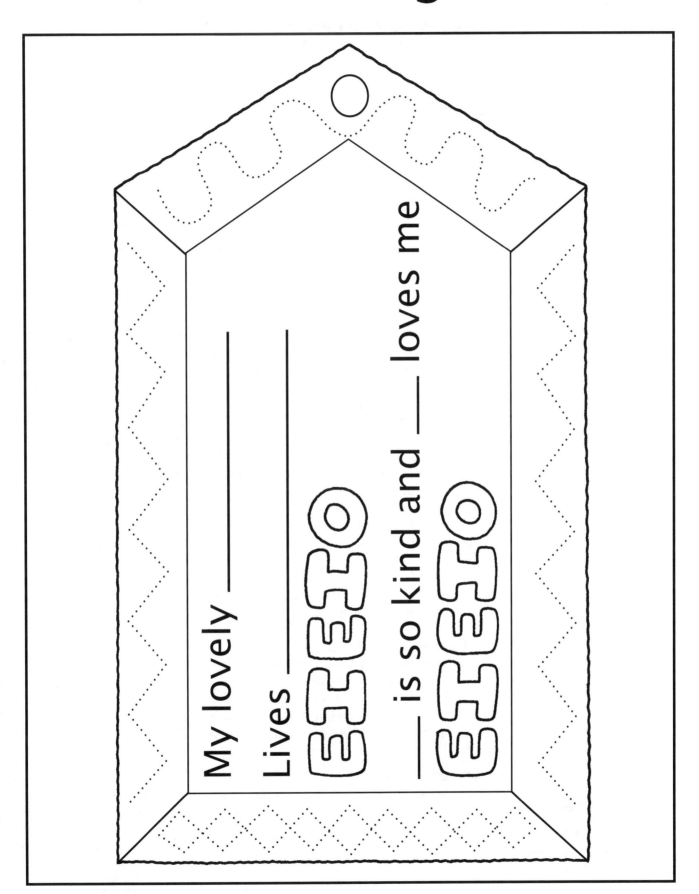

Maths

Removal workers

STEPPING STONE
Sometimes show confidence and offer solutions to problems.

EARLY LEARNING GOAL
Begin to relate addition to combining two groups of objects and subtraction to 'taking away'. (MD)

ASSESSMENT
Are the children gaining the confidence to offer solutions to simple mathematical problems?

What you need
One large and one small cardboard box; masking tape; paint; paintbrushes; scissors (for adult use); old wooden or plastic brick; several items of toy furniture.

Preparation
An adult should cut two large flaps in one end of the large box to represent van doors.

What to do
Talk to the children about the role of removal workers and how they help us to pack up and transport our items when we move from one house to the next.

Invite the children to make a model of a removal van by taping a small cardboard box, representing the drivers' cab, on to the front of a large box. Encourage the children to paint the model and to decorate the sides with the words, 'Removal van'. When dry, ask the children to fill the model van with toy furniture.

Next, help the children to make a dice by labelling an old wooden or plastic brick with the numbers: −1, −2, −3, −4, +1, +2. Invite the children to take turns to throw the dice. If the dice shows, say '−2', then that child should carefully remove two items of furniture from the van. If the dice shows, say '+1', then that child must replace an item of furniture. If a player has no items to replace, the dice is passed on to the next player. As they play, encourage the children to use the language of addition and subtraction to explain what they are doing.

Continue playing until the van is empty. The player with the most pieces of furniture is the winner. Alternatively, just play for fun.

Discussion
Talk about the meaning of mathematical terms such as 'add', 'plus', 'one more', 'three extra', 'take-away' and 'minus'.

Follow-up activities
● Help the children to complete photocopiable page 17, 'The removal van' by counting and writing how many items are left inside the removal van.
● Encourage the children to adapt the game by adding or taking away toy furniture from a dolls' house.

Differentiation
Help younger children to make a dice showing the numbers: −1, −1, −1, −1, +1, +1. Invite older children to play the game using 20 items of toy furniture.

ON THE CD-ROM
● Photocopiable sheet 'The removal van'

The removal van

themes for early years

Mark-making

A helpful invention

What you need
Clipboard; paper; felt-tipped pens; books or pictures showing a variety of different types and uses of electric light; books or pictures showing other forms of light such as sunlight, moonlight, candles and flares; photocopiable page 19, 'We see the light'.

What to do
Invite the children to look at a variety of books and pictures showing different types of light. Talk about the differences between the forms of light. Now ask the children to imagine how people coped before there was any electric light. What did they do when it got dark?

Talk about Thomas Edison and his team, and explain that they helped us by inventing the electric light. Help the children to appreciate the impact of the invention by challenging them to find out if all the rooms in your setting have an electric light.

Give each group of children a copy of photocopiable page 19, 'We see the light' attached to a clipboard. Help them to write the words 'yes' and 'no' at the top of the page and the name of five different rooms in your setting in the left hand column, for example, 'Hall', 'Our room', 'Art cupboard', 'Cloakroom'.

Ask the children to create a simple 'yes/no' tally by walking around the building, ticking 'yes' or 'no' on their sheet depending on whether or not each room has a light.

When they have finished, talk about the results. Explain that, before the electric light was invented, people would have used candles or oil lamps to help them see in the dark. Ask the children to consider why a candle might not be as safe or as useful as an electric light.

Discussion
Talk to parents and carers about the activity and ask them to help their child to repeat the tally challenge at home. Invite the children to bring in their tally sheets and to talk about the results.

> ### Follow-up activity
> ● Help the children to count how many different types of light there are in and around your setting, for example, torches, table lamps, fluorescent lights, street lamps and security lights.

Differentiation
Walk around the building with younger or less able children. Invite older or more able children to complete the tally individually or in pairs.

ON THE CD-ROM
● Photocopiable sheet 'We see the light'

People who help us

We see the light

Rooms	yes	no
1		
2		
3		
4		
5		

Sound

themes for early years

Neighbours

What you need
Percussion instruments.

What to do
Talk to the children about helpful neighbours or friendly people who live nearby. Note relevant comments such as, 'I have tea at Rosie's house when my mummy works' or 'I play at Sam's when Toby goes to the clinic' or 'Alison feeds our dog when we stay with Nana'.

Encourage the children to talk about these helpful or friendly neighbours by making up short songs. For example:

> *Rosie is my neighbour, neighbour, neighbour.*
> *Rosie is my neighbour and she helps me.*
> *I have tea with Rosie, Rosie, Rosie,*
> *I have tea with Rosie and she helps me.*
> *Sam is my neighbour, neighbour, neighbour.*
> *Sam is my neighbour and he helps me.*
> *Sam and I like playing, playing, playing;*
> *Sam and I like playing and he is friends with me.*
> *Alison is our neighbour, neighbour, neighbour.*
> *Alison is our neighbour and she helps us.*
> *Rover goes to Alison's, Alison's, Alison's;*
> *Rover goes to Alison's and she is friends with us.*

When the children are familiar with the new words, encourage them to clap rhythmically as they sing. After you have sung and clapped the rhythm of songs a few times, provide some percussion instruments for the children to play while they sing.

Discussion
Provide an opportunity for the children to perform their favourite song or instrument to an 'audience' and to explain why they like it.

Follow-up activities
- Encourage the children to paint pictures to illustrate the words in the new songs.
- Invite the children to make up hand actions or short dance sequences to accompany the new songs.
- Sing the song 'Friends and neighbours' on page 79 or listen to it on the CD-ROM.

Differentiation
Help younger or less able children by introducing different aspects of this activity during different sessions. For example, sing the song during the first session, introduce rhythmic clapping during the second session and incorporate percussion instruments during the third session. Encourage older or more able children to use a tape recorder to record the songs and music.

STEPPING STONE
Sing to themselves and make up simple songs.

EARLY LEARNING GOAL
Recognise and explore how sounds can be changed, sing simple songs from memory, recognise repeated sounds and sound patterns and match movements to music. (CD)

ASSESSMENT
Do the children have the confidence to sing simple songs from memory? Are they happy to explore how sounds, and words, to simple songs can be changed?

ON THE CD-ROM
- Song 'Friends and neighbours'

People who help us

Helping in our setting

When children start attending an early years setting their horizons broaden and they encounter a wider range of 'people who help us'.

Special helpers

Food

STEPPING STONE
Sustain interest for a length of time on a pre-decided construction or arrangement.

EARLY LEARNING GOAL
Use language such as 'greater', 'smaller', 'heavier' or 'lighter' to compare quantities. (MD)

ASSESSMENT
Are the children gaining an awareness of mathematical terms such as 'greater', 'smaller', 'heavier' or 'lighter' to compare quantities?

What you need
Ingredients: 50g self-raising flour, 50g caster sugar, 50g butter or margarine, one egg; Decoration: icing sugar, warm water, small sweets or candied peel; Equipment: plastic mixing bowls, weighing scales, spoons, forks, small lined cake tins – 15–20cm in diameter; poem 'Here comes the caretaker' on page 93 or the CD-ROM; photograph of the school cooks from the CD-ROM.

Preparation
Check with parents or carers for any food allergies or dietry requirements before commencing this activity. Ask the children to wash their hands and to put on aprons. Pre-heat oven to 180˚C.

What to do
Invite the children to make a cake for a special helper, of their choice, to say 'Thank you'. Share the poem 'Here comes the caretaker' on page 93, and look at the photograph of the school cooks.

Help each child to weigh the ingredients. Encourage them to use mathematical language as they do so. Support the children when breaking the egg into a bowl and then mix all of the ingredients together. When mixed, let the children spoon the mixture into the cake tin. An adult should put the cake in the oven for 15–20 minutes, until golden brown. Once cooked, leave it to cool on a wire rack.

Help the children to mix two tablespoons of icing sugar with warm water to create a thick, smooth paste. Invite them to spread the icing on to their cake and to add other decorations.

Discussion
Talk about other types of food that is used as a gift.

Follow-up activity
● Provide each child with a small cake box to decorate.

Differentiation
Work with younger or less able children individually. Let older or more able children use small tubes of coloured icing to decorate their cake with the name of the person who helps them.

ON THE CD-ROM
● Poem 'Here comes the caretaker'
● Photograph of school cooks

Group helpers

themes for early years

STEPPING STONE
Have a sense of belonging.

EARLY LEARNING GOAL
Respond to significant experiences, showing a range of feelings when appropriate. (PSED)

ASSESSMENT
Do the children respond to comments and questions by explaining or showing a range of feelings?

What you need
Long strip of paper, such as plain wallpaper; felt-tipped pens; paints; paintbrushes; paper; sticky labels or paper; glue.

What to do
Talk to the children about the different ways that the adults in your setting help them. Ask questions such as: *Who helps you to cook? What does (Mrs May) help you to do? Does anyone help you in the library?*

Lay out the strip of wallpaper on the floor and ask a willing adult helper, such as a group assistant or parent helper, to lie down on the paper. Invite the children to draw around the helper, taking turns to draw around different parts of the helper's body. Encourage the children to fill the outline with paint, including features and details such as eyes, nose, mouth, hair, clothes and shoes.

Ask the children to suggest some positive comments about the helpers in your setting. For example, they could say 'Our helpers are kind'; 'Our helpers are funny'; 'Our helpers look after us' or 'Our helpers read to us'. Help the children to label the life-sized portrait with the comments.

Discussion
Talk to the children about their favourite activities, games or part of the day. How do the helpers in your setting help to make these sessions so special? Ask the children to describe some of the things that helpers in your setting do. Would they like to do all these tasks? What sort of job would they like to do when they are adults?

Follow-up activities
● Display the life-sized portrait in a prominent position for the children to observe, read and discuss.
● Invite the children to take a photograph of each helper (with their permission) or draw pictures to mount on separate copies of photocopiable page 23, 'Thank you'. Help the children to write 'thank you' in the space above the picture and the name of the helper in the space below the picture. The side panels can be decorated with colourful patterns. Display the framed pictures in the entrance of your setting.

Differentiation
Help younger or less able children by scribing the positive comments on to large labels for them to stick in position. Encourage older or more able children to write the labels using emergent writing or copy writing.

ON THE CD-ROM
● Photocopiable sheet 'Thank you'

Thank you

themes for early years

Our dinner supervisor

STEPPING STONE
Use words and/or gestures, including body language such as eye contact and facial expression, to communicate.

EARLY LEARNING GOAL
Interact with others, negotiating plans and activities and taking turns in conversation. (CLL)

ASSESSMENT
Do the children take turns in conversation and cooperate with their peers during the book making activity?

What you need
Strip of card; squares of plain paper; felt-tipped pens; coloured pencils; glue.

Preparation
Fold the strip of card backwards and forwards to create a blank zigzag booklet.

What to do
Talk to the children about the different ways in which they are helped by the dinner supervisor in your setting. Ask questions, such as: *Who looks after you at lunch time? Does anyone help you to open your lunch box? How does (Mrs Jones) help you in the playground?*

Provide the children with paper and pens, and encourage them to draw simple pictures showing the dinner supervisor helping them at lunchtime. Write the words '(Name of dinner supervisor) helps us to' on the front cover of the zigzag book, and then invite the children to glue the pictures on the remaining pages.

Help the children to label each picture with a short caption explaining the ways in which the dinner supervisor helps them. For example, '(Mrs Jones) helps us to... open our lunch box; collect our coats; play in the playground'.

Discussion
Look through the book with the children and encourage them to take turns to talk about their picture.

Follow-up activities
- Display the children's book in the book corner with a collection of commercial books about people who help us.
- The children could paint pictures on to large sheets of paper, to compile into a giant zigzag book. Alternatively, hang the paintings in the dinner area as colourful mobiles.
- Invite the children to complete photocopiable page 25, 'On Monday I ate' by drawing real or imaginary foods for each day. Cut out the pictures and display in the correct order to create a mini picture-booklet.
- Allow the children to complete the on-screen activity 'Healthy lunch box'.

Differentiation
Scribe the words for younger or less able children. Encourage older or more able children to write their captions on the computer. Help them to print out the words, and then cut them out and to stick them in the correct order in the zigzag book.

ON THE CD-ROM
- Photocopiable sheet 'On Monday I ate'
- On-screen activity 'Healthy lunch box'

On Monday I ate

On Wednesday I ate	At the weekend I ate
On Tuesday I ate	On Friday I ate
On Monday I ate	On Thursday I ate

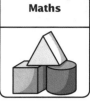

Maths

Our caretaker

What you need
Photocopiable page 27, 'Counting caretaker'; felt-tipped pens; coloured pencils; a friendly caretaker; poem 'Here comes the caretaker' on page 93 or on the CD-ROM.

Preparation
If possible, invite the caretaker to talk to the children about his or her duties and responsibilities and to take the children on a guided tour around your setting to explain what goes on 'behind the scenes'.

What to do
Talk to the children about the role of the caretaker in your setting and read the poem 'Here comes the caretaker' on page 93, or listen to it on the CD-ROM. During or following the caretaker's tour, ask the children practical questions, relevant to your setting. For example: *How many brooms can you see in the cupboard? Does the caretaker unlock more than two doors in the morning? How many sinks and how many taps need cleaning?*

Give each child a copy of photocopiable page 27, 'Counting caretaker'. Explain that they have to look very carefully at the picture to see how many of each item they can find. Once they have counted the number of, for example, mops, they should write the correct number in the box at the bottom of the sheet. As they find each item, invite the children to colour it in.

Discussion
Talk about different day-to-day activities that often involve counting, for example, counting the number of chairs at a table, brushes in the paint pot, aprons in the craft area.

> ### Follow-up activities
> ● Hide two sets of labels, showing the numbers one to five or one to ten, in easy to find locations around your setting. Help the children to develop skills in number recognition by taking them on a guided tour around your setting to find and match the hidden numbers.
> ● Repeat the above activity, but this time help the children to develop skills in addition by asking them to find and add two of the numbers hidden in your setting.

Differentiation
Help younger or less able children by providing an enlarged copy of the photocopiable sheet for the whole group to use together. Encourage older or more able children to develop skills in addition by asking them questions related to the photocopiable sheet. For example: *How many brooms and mops can you see? How many large and small brushes are there in the picture? How many pots altogether?*

themes for early years

STEPPING STONE
Show an interest in numbers and counting.

EARLY LEARNING GOAL
Say and use number names in order in familiar contexts. (MD)

ASSESSMENT
Are the children able to say and use number names, in order, in familiar contexts?

ON THE CD-ROM
● Photocopiable sheet 'Counting caretaker'
● Poem 'Here comes the caretaker'

Counting caretaker

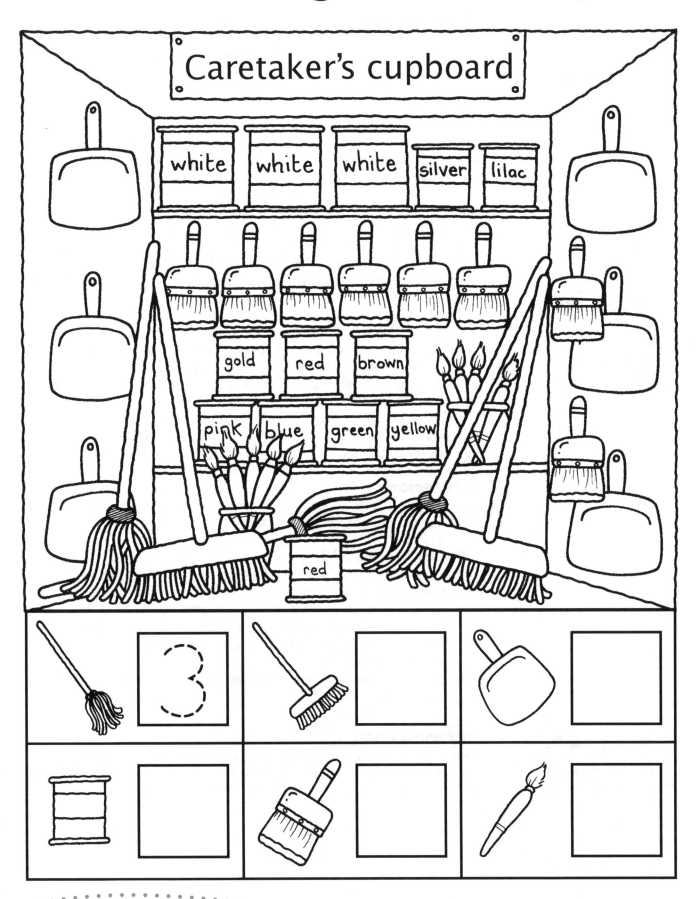

Caretaker's cupboard

white white white silver lilac

gold red brown

pink blue green yellow

red

themes for early years

Our cook

STEPPING STONE
Show awareness of own needs with regard to eating, sleeping and hygiene.

EARLY LEARNING GOAL
Recognise the importance of keeping healthy and those things which contribute to this. (PD)

ASSESSMENT
Are the children beginning to recognise the importance of keeping healthy and those things that contribute to this?

What you need
Salt dough (or clay); clay boards or mats; poster or acrylic paints; painting equipment; PVA glue; examples of real fruit and vegetables; photograph of school cooks from the CD-ROM.

What to do
Help the children to find out about the role of the cook in your setting. If possible, visit the kitchen area or invite the cook to talk to the children about the meals that they prepare. Look together at the photograph of the school cooks.

Alternatively, talk to the children about food preparation at home and encourage them to describe their favourite foods. Talk to the children about the importance of eating healthy foods, such as fruit and vegetables. Ask the children to describe their favourite fruits and vegetables or favourite dishes containing fruit or vegetables.

Provide the children with some salt dough and invite them to create pretend items of healthy food. Display examples of real food nearby for the children to use as visual aids while they are making their models.

When dry, invite the children to paint the items to make them look realistic. When the paint is dry, help the children to varnish the models by applying a thin coat of PVA glue. When the glue is dry it creates a clear, hard, shiny surface that protects the paint from flaking off when the items are handled.

Invite the children to use the pretend food in the home corner for role play situations based on cooking, eating and buying or selling food. For example, you could have a pretend kitchen, café or market stall.

Discussion
Talk with the children about general issues of personal hygiene, for example, washing hands before handling food and before meals.

Follow-up activities
● The children could cut out colourful magazine pictures showing fruit and vegetables to create a 'healthy' food collage.
● Ask the children to complete photocopiable page 29, 'Five a day' by matching the pictures to the appropriate name and initial letter. Talk about the benefits of eating five different fruits and vegetables each day.
● Allow the children to complete the on-screen activity 'Healthy lunch box'.

Differentiation
Help younger or less able children during the model-making stage. Encourage older or more able children to mix their own paint colours to make their models as realistic as possible.

ON THE CD-ROM
● Photocopiable sheet 'Five a day'
● Photograph of school cooks
● On-screen activity 'Healthy lunch box'

Five a day

b		apple
a		banana
t		carrot
o		orange
c		tomato

themes for early years

STEPPING STONE
Explore malleable materials by patting, stroking, poking, squeezing, pinching and twisting them.

EARLY LEARNING GOAL
Handle tools, objects, construction and malleable materials safely and with increasing control. (PD)

ASSESSMENT
Are the children able to handle model-making tools and malleable materials with care and control?

Our secretary

What you need
Air-drying clay; clay boards or mats; hand-washing facilities; poster or acrylic paints; paintbrushes; paper; dried flowers.

Preparation
If possible, take the children to visit the secretary in his or her office at your setting.

What to do
Invite the children to work as a team to make a vase for the secretary's desk. Talk about why they are making the vase, for example, to brighten the office or to say 'thank you' for everything that the secretary does for you.

Provide the children with small lumps of air-drying clay and ask them to roll it gently to create long thin sausage shapes. Help them to wind the first few sausage shapes into a tight, flat coil to create the base of a vase. Next, help them to gradually add extra coils to the outside edge of the base to create a rim.

Encourage the children to gradually build the sides of the vase by taking turns to add further coils to the rim. Keep going until the children are happy with the shape and size of their vase.

When dry, invite the children to take turns to paint the ridged surface in several different colours to create a stripy vase. When complete, place some dried flowers in the vase to present to the secretary. (Do not fill with water and use fresh flowers, as the vase will not be waterproof.)

Discussion
Talk to the children about how the secretary helps the staff, parents and children in your setting by, for example, checking the registers, answering the telephone and writing letters.

Follow-up activities
● Show the children how to add a textured pattern to the clay vase using a plastic fork.
● Divide the vase into sections, patchwork style, using a soft pencil. Invite the children to take turns to paint one section each using their own choice of colours.

Differentiation
Help younger or less able children by providing hand-over-hand support during the modelling stage. Encourage older or more able children to smooth the coils on the outside edge of the vase before painting it with pictures, shapes or patterns.

ICT

themes for early years

We help visitors

What you need
Computer with a colour printer; A4 paper in various colours; display board near the entrance to your setting; coloured backing paper; coloured pens and pencils; scissors; glue.

Preparation
Cover the display board with colourful backing paper.

What to do
Explain to the children that you are going to make an information board to help visitors to your setting. Help each child to write the word 'Welcome' using the computer. Show the children how to change the font size and colour of the writing and then show each child how to print a copy of the word on to A4 paper.

Invite the children to use coloured pens and pencils to create a decorative border around their printed word. Next, help each child to cut around the outside edge of their sheet to make a decorative border for their 'Welcome' sign. Encourage the children to glue the 'Welcome' signs around the edges of the display board.

Ask the children to think of useful information that could be placed in the centre of the display board to help visitors. For example, you could include the name of your setting, the names of the staff, the start and finish times and the current theme or topic that you are exploring.

Help the children to write this information on the computer and to print it out on to sheets of coloured paper. Encourage them to add this information to the display board to create a simple 'Welcome and Information' board for visitors to your setting.

Discussion
Talk about other languages used by people in your community. Invite parents and carers of children who speak English as a second language into your setting to help their child write the word 'Welcome' on the computer in their first language.

Follow-up activities
● Invite the children to take photographs of the adults who work in your setting to display on the poster (with their permission).
● Alternatively, invite the children to display photographs of interesting features within your setting, such as the nature plot, the music corner or the play area.

Differentiation
Provide younger or less able children with one-to-one assistance. Give computer literate children an opportunity to share their skills with adults or peers in your setting.

Let's all help

What you need
Two circles of card (approximately 50cm and 30cm in diameter); a split-pin paper fastener; coloured pens and pencils; black felt-tipped pen.

Preparation
Create a simple blank spinner by dividing both circles of card into four sections using a black felt-tipped pen. Place the small circle on top of the large circle and secure them together using a split-pin paper fastener. Make sure that the small circle of card spins freely.

What to do
Talk to the children about how they can become 'helpers' or 'cleaners' in your setting by taking it in turns to do jobs such as, cleaning the paintbrushes, tidying the bookshelf, feeding the goldfish and collecting the PE equipment.

Show the children the blank spinner and explain that they are going to turn it into a 'Helping-hands wheel'. Ask the children to draw a picture of the four helpful jobs in the four outer sections of the spinner. Next, ask each child to write their name in one of the four sections of the inner wheel.

Place the 'Helping hands wheel' in a prominent position. Encourage the children to take turns to spin the wheel to find out who is doing each job when the need arises.

Discussion
Talk to the children about the different ways in which they help the staff in your setting. Ask questions such as: *Which helpful jobs do you enjoy most? Which job is the least fun? Are there any new jobs you would like to do to help?*

Follow-up activities
- Help two or three children to write their names in each section of the inner wheel so that different groups of children will have responsibility for each job instead of individuals.
- Help the children to write their first and second names on the inner wheel.
- Share the poem 'There was an old woman' on page 92.

Differentiation
Help younger or less able children to copy write their name. Encourage older or more able children to write short captions describing the four jobs instead of drawing four pictures.

ON THE CD-ROM
- Poem 'There was an old woman'

People who help us

Keeping us healthy

This chapter introduces the wide range of people who help keep us healthy or treat us when we are ill. Some children will have encountered these people and can share their experiences.

themes for early years

Nurses

Role play

What you need
Room with enough space for the children to move freely and safely; A4 paper; thick black pen; access to a photocopier; whistle or buzzer; PE mat; photograph of a nurse from the CD-ROM.

What to do
Invite the children to draw four pictures, on separate pieces of paper, showing a man, a woman, a boy and a girl. Photocopy each picture.

Place one picture in each corner of the room to represent four patients. Choose one child to sit on a PE mat in the centre of the room, and put the photocopied pictures face down in front of that child. Tell the remaining children that they are going to pretend to be nurses rushing around a hospital helping all the patients.

Start by asking the children to move around the room, dodging each other as they pretend to visit each patient. After a short time, blow a whistle or press the buzzer to indicate that one of the patients needs attention. On hearing this, the children should each stand by a patient.

Invite the child on the PE mat to reveal one of the photocopied pictures. All of the nurses standing beside this patient should sit down. Ask the child in the centre to shuffle the pictures and put them on the mat, face down. The children who are left standing should carry on playing the game in the same way. Continue play until all of the children are seated beside a patient.

Discussion
Look at the photograph of a nurse and ask the children if they can tell you what nurses do. Does anyone know where nurses work?

Follow-up activities
- Sing the song 'Whose hat is that?' on page 84 and share the poem 'Visiting the nurse' on page 94.
- Adapt the game by having four pictures showing houses. The children can pretend to be nurses rushing from house to house.

Differentiation
With younger or less able children, play the game in small groups. Encourage older or more able children to move around the room while balancing a small ball on a plastic spoon to represent a tablet.

ON THE CD-ROM
- Photograph of a nurse
- Song 'Whose hat is that?'
- Poem 'Visiting the nurse'

Role play

themes for early years

Doctors and surgeons

STEPPING STONE
Show an interest in the world in which they live.

EARLY LEARNING GOAL
Find out about their environment, and talk about those features they like and dislike. (KUW)

ASSESSMENT
Do the children show signs of curiosity and interest in the world around them by asking questions, joining in conversations and listening to the experiences of others?

What you need
Toy bed or couch; toy dolls or teddy bears; doll blankets; tables; magazines or comics; chairs; telephone; paper; pencils; doctor's dressing-up outfit or a white shirt; real or toy stethoscope; bandages; scissors; cotton wool; photocopiable page 35, 'I can'.

What to do
Talk to the children about how doctors and surgeons help us. Encourage the children to recall times when they have visited or been visited by a doctor.

Invite the children to help you set up a 'Doctor's surgery' in the role-play area. Include features such as a waiting room with chairs and a small table displaying comics or magazines, a reception area with a telephone, paper and pencils and a consulting room with a table, two chairs, a couch, blankets, bandages, scissors and cotton wool.

Suggest that the children dress up as doctors for role play situations that involve helping injured and sick toys. Encourage them to pretend to write prescriptions, to listen to the toys' chests with the stethoscope and to bandage the toys' damaged limbs.

Encourage the 'doctors' to write imaginary notes about each patient and to create pretend prescriptions for the ill toys. Invite the children who are pretending to be receptionists to create appointments and to record the toys' names and dates of birth.

Discussion
Use photocopiable page 35, 'I can' to inspire discussion about daily routines that help to keep their bodies clean and healthy. Encourage the children to identify the routines that they can do independently or enjoy the most, for example, eating fresh fruit and vegetables, exercising, washing hands, bathing, brushing their hair and brushing their teeth.

Follow-up activities
- Create other role-play areas relevant to health, such as a baby clinic, a chemist's shop, an optician's or a dentist's surgery.
- Encourage the children to make some 'Get Well' cards for the toys in the role-play area or for the children who are off sick.
- Sing the song 'Guess who?' together on page 82 or listen to it on the CD-ROM.

Differentiation
Help younger or less able children by encouraging them to join in role play situations with older children. Encourage older or more able children to write simple labels for the pretend surgery, for example, 'Waiting room', 'Dr Jane's room', 'Please sit here' and 'Collect your prescription here'.

ON THE CD-ROM
- Photocopiable sheet 'I can'
- Song 'Guess who?'

People who help us

I can

Art and craft

themes for early years

The dentist

What you need
Four sheets of A4 white card; one sheet of A1 pink card; scissors; glue; sticky tape; a display board at the children's own height; poem 'The dentist' on page 88 or on the CD-ROM; song 'Meet my dentist' on page 84 or on the CD-ROM; photograph of a dentist from the CD-ROM.

Preparation
Share or listen to the song 'Meet my dentist' on page 84 and the poem 'The dentist' on page 88 with the children and talk about the children's experiences of having their teeth looked at by the dentist.

What to do
Observe the photograph of a dentist on the CD-ROM. Explain that the dentist helps us by checking that our teeth are strong and healthy.

Help the children to trim the edges off four sheets of A4 white card to create four large teeth shapes. Next, help them to cut two giant, smiling lip shapes from pink card. Glue the lips to the top and bottom edges of the four giant teeth to represent a huge smiley mouth. Explain that the shape of the teeth and lips does not need to be accurate, in fact the funnier the better!

Attach the smiley mouth to a display board at the children's own height. Help the children to decorate the display with drawings, painting and magazine pictures that focus on keeping teeth healthy, visiting the dentist and tooth care products.

Discussion
Use the display to inspire discussion about visiting the dentist and everyday dental hygiene routines, such as brushing teeth regularly, brushing them properly and not eating too many sugary foods between meals.

Follow-up activities
- Help the children to create a giant 3D model of a toothbrush to add to your display. Paint a long cardboard box, such as a baking foil box. When dry, an adult should cut an oval hole in the base of the box so that the children can push the bristles of a dustpan brush through the hole. Tape the brush handle firmly to the inside of the box using strong tape. Place the giant toothbrush in front of your display.
- Create a giant toothbrush holder for the toothbrush by taping coloured card around an old, clean bucket or waste-paper bin. Invite the children to decorate the holder with stripes, dots or patterns using paints or sticky paper.
- Listen to the song 'Guess who?' on the CD-ROM, also on page 82.

Differentiation
Draw the shapes of the teeth and lips on to the card for younger children to cut around. Encourage older or more able children to add relevant labels to the display.

STEPPING STONE
Work creatively on a large or small scale.

EARLY LEARNING GOAL
Explore colour, texture, shape, form and space in two or three dimensions. (CD)

ASSESSMENT
Are the children keen to help create a shared display by incorporating their work and ideas with the work and ideas of others?

ON THE CD-ROM
- Photograph of a dentist
- Poem 'The dentist'
- Song 'Meet my dentist'
- Song 'Guess who?'

People who help us

Construction and malleable materials

Healthy feet

STEPPING STONE
Engage in activities requiring hand-eye coordination.

EARLY LEARNING GOAL
Handle tools, objects, construction and malleable materials safely and with increasing control. (PD)

ASSESSMENT
Are the children developing skills in hand-eye coordination?

What you need
Cardboard; scissors; bradawl (adult use); shoelaces or thick wool; pens; crayons; dice showing dots or numbers one to six; on-screen activity 'Fairytale shoe shop' from the CD-ROM.

Preparation
An adult should cut out a cardboard shoe-print for each child and pierce six holes (two rows of three) on each side, to represent shoelace eyelets. Invite the children to complete the on-screen activity 'Fairytale shoe shop'.

What to do
Give each child a cardboard shoe-print and ask them to number the holes from one to six on both sides (the numbers on each side do not need to match, for example, hole number 'two' could be labelled 'five' on the opposite side.) Encourage the children to decorate the shape using pens or crayons to represent a shoe. Give each child a shoelace or length of thick wool, knotted at one end.

Invite pairs of children to use the shoe shapes and shoelaces to play a shoelace tying game. Ask the first player to throw a dice. If, say, a four is shown, then that player should thread their lace through one of the holes numbered four. If a thread is already in hole four, then that player misses a turn. The dice is then passed to the next player.

Continue taking turns to throw the dice and thread the lace. The winner is the first player to run out of lace. Alternatively, just play for fun.

Discussion
Talk to the children about shoe shops and shoe-shop assistants. Ask questions such as: *Who helps the customers in a shoe shop? How are feet measured? Who measures them? Who helps you to tie your laces?*

Follow-up activities
● Set up a shoe shop in the role-play area and encourage the children to pretend they are shoe-shop assistants and customers.
● Help the children to practise tying a bow or a simple knot using the laces in the cardboard shoe shapes.
● Share the song 'Guess who?' on page 82.

Differentiation
Write the numbers on the shoe shapes for younger or less able children. Encourage older or more able children to make two dice by labelling two wooden bricks with the numbers one to three. Ask the children to throw both dice and add the score to find out which hole to thread their shoelace.

ON THE CD-ROM
● On-screen activity 'Fairytale shoe shop'
● Song 'Guess who?'

Opticians

STEPPING STONE
Value and contribute to own well-being and self-control.

EARLY LEARNING GOAL
Form good relationships with adults and peers. (PSED)

ASSESSMENT
Do the children have the confidence to work alongside adults and peers during role play?

What you need
Pipe-cleaners in several colours; safety mirror; photocopiable page 39, 'Snap!' copied onto card; sticky tape; poem 'I had a pair of glasses' on page 93 or on the CD-ROM.

What to do
Talk with the children about what opticians do and how they can help us. Encourage them to share first-hand experiences of visiting an optician or choosing glasses. Invite the children to join in with the poem, 'I had a pair of glasses' on page 93.

Provide an assortment of colourful pipe-cleaners and show the children how to twist and bend them together to create pretend glasses in humorous shapes and sizes. (Make sure that there are no sharp ends on the pipe-cleaners by sealing them with a small piece of tape.)

Display the pretend glasses together with a mirror in the role-play area, and encourage the children to wear them during imaginative play. Ask them to describe and compare the different shapes and colours of the pretend glasses, then challenge them further by inviting them to find a pair of pretend glasses to suit each adult in your setting.

Discussion
Give the children with two A4 or two A3 card copies of photocopiable page 39, 'Snap!' and invite them to colour in and cut out the pictures to create eight playing cards showing funny-looking glasses. Talk about the pictures and use them to play matching games such as 'snap' and 'pairs'.

Follow-up activities
● Provide collage materials and decorative accessories such as card, coloured feathers, sequins, beads and shiny paper and invite the children to create large fancy dress or pantomime style glasses.
● Encourage the children to do illustrations for the words in the poem 'I had a pair of glasses' on page 93. Display the pictures on the wall with an enlarged copy of the poem.

Differentiation
Help younger or less able children to bend and shape the pipe-cleaners. Encourage older or more able children to make the pretend glasses using the colours mentioned in the poem: orange, black, green, pink and red.

ON THE CD-ROM
● Poem 'I had a pair of glasses'
● Photocopiable sheet 'Snap!'

Snap!

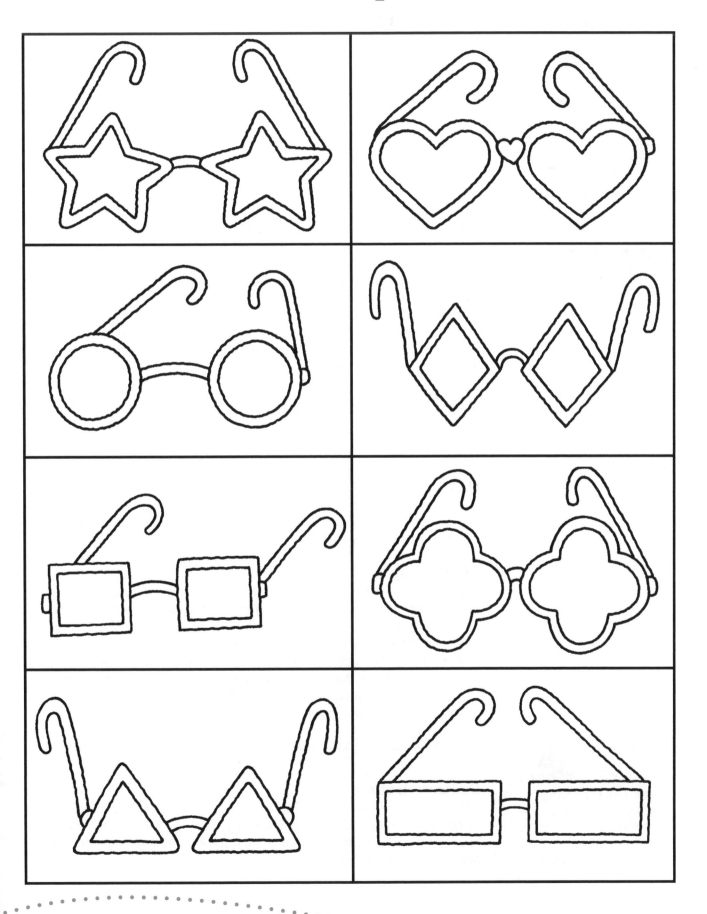

themes for early years

Hair care

STEPPING STONE
Show an awareness of change.

EARLY LEARNING GOAL
Look closely at similarities, differences, patterns and change. (KUW)

ASSESSMENT
Do the children show an awareness of change by means of discussion and description?

What you need
Large sheets of thick paper or card; felt-tipped pens; colourful collage materials such as wool, braid, crêpe paper, tissue, fabric, ribbon, shredded paper, shredded Cellophane, string and cotton wool; glue; sticky tape; poem 'Haircut' on page 88 or on the CD-ROM; photograph of a hairdresser from the CD-ROM.

Preparation
If possible, arrange to visit a local hairdressing salon or invite a hairdresser into your setting to talk to the children about their work.

What to do
Say the poem 'Haircut' on page 88 or listen to it on the CD-ROM and look at the photograph of a hairdresser. Invite the children to imagine that they are a hairdresser who creates wild hair styles! Talk about the changes that they could make to their own hair, for example: What colour would they choose? What style would they like? Would they like to wear hair extensions, braids or wigs?

Help the children to draw a bold smiling face on the bottom half of a large sheet of card or thick paper, then encourage them to create a collage showing a wild wig or 'hair do' using a range of colourful, textured materials.

Invite the children to adapt and change their ideas as they work, for example, adding extra colours to the hair, changing the length by incorporating more materials and altering the shape to make it look wider, higher or more wild!

Discussion
Explore the theme of 'change' by talking about changes in nature, for example, the change in our appearance as we grow, seasonal changes and changes in the weather.

Follow-up activities
● Use the children's collages to decorate the role-play area to represent a funky hairdressing salon. Provide old wigs or dolls for the children to decorate with ribbons, braids, clips, slides combs and other jazzy accessories.
● Help the children cover balloons with papier mâché. When dry, invite the children to paint and decorate the 3D shape to represent a clown's head with a wild hair do.
● Collect photographs of family or friends showing changing hairstyles.
● Share the song 'Guess who?' on page 82.

ON THE CD-ROM
● Photograph of a hairdresser
● Poem 'Haircut'
● Song 'Guess who?'

Differentiation
Help younger or less able children with the practical challenges such as cutting, taping and glueing. Encourage older or more able children to create a collage with a colour theme, for example, wigs in shades of blue and purple or red and orange.

A health pioneer

STEPPING STONE
Show some understanding that good practices with regard to exercise, eating, sleeping and hygiene can contribute to good health.

EARLY LEARNING GOAL
Recognise the importance of keeping healthy and those things which contribute to this. (PD)

ASSESSMENT
Are the children gaining an awareness of how they can help themselves with regard to living a healthy lifestyle?

What you need
Books about Florence Nightingale, healthy food and hygiene; large sheet of paper or card; felt-tipped pens; pencils; small sheets of paper; glue; song 'People who helped us' on page 86 or on the CD-ROM.

What to do
Talk to the children about the legacy of Florence Nightingale and join in with the song 'People who helped us' on page 86 or listen to it on the CD-ROM. Explain that she was a nurse who worked hard to improve patient care. She is particularly famous for helping injured soldiers and making other medical workers aware of the importance of hygiene when treating wounds and sickness.

She became known as the 'Lady of the lamp' because she carried an oil lamp so she could check the welfare of her patients in the dark. Florence Nightingale's dedication helped many people in the past to survive illness and injury and her ideas have continued to help us to this very day.

Ask the children to talk about issues of hygiene by encouraging them to consider why we should wash our hands before handling food or after visiting the toilet. Talk about other actions we should take to help prevent spreading illness, for example, covering our mouth when we sneeze or cough and throwing away dirty tissues.

Invite them to draw pictures to illustrate these points. Help the children to glue their pictures on to a large sheet of card or paper, collage style, to create a pictorial chart showing good practices with regard to exercise, eating, sleeping and hygiene. Display the chart in a prominent position with relevant books and posters nearby.

Discussion
Ask the children to think of other things that we can do to keep us fit and healthy, for example, taking exercise, eating sensibly and getting enough sleep.

Follow-up activities
● Encourage the children to suggest and join in with physical challenges for fun, such as setting up an obstacle course, devising simple team games or playing traditional games such as hopscotch and skipping.
● Supervise the children as they use the internet to find out more information about Florence Nightingale.

Differentiation
Help younger or less able children to cut out pictures from magazines to glue on to the chart. Invite older or more able children to write relevant labels or captions to glue next to each picture.

ON THE CD-ROM
● Song 'People who helped us'

Small-world play

Healthy pets

What you need
Long sheet of card; thick marker pens; a box; six small toy animals; four play people; a dice; photograph of a vet from the CD-ROM.

What to do
Look at the photograph of a vet with the children and talk about how vets can help us to care for our pets and other animals. Involve the children in making a thought-provoking floor game that involves decision-making skills and an awareness of what is right and what is wrong regarding animal welfare.

Help the children to draw a pathway along a strip of card. Divide the path into 20 to 30 sections. Write 'Home' in the first section and 'Fairground' in the last section. Encourage them to draw windows, a door and a 'red cross' sign on to a cardboard box to represent a vet's surgery. Place this near to the pathway.

Ask the children to place six small toy animals randomly on the pathway. Explain that these represent injured animals. Give each child a toy figure to use as a counter, and ask them to place these in the space labelled 'Home'.

Invite the first child to throw the dice. If, for example, a five is shown, then that player should move their play figure forward five spaces towards the fair. If the figure lands on a space occupied by an injured animal, the player must make a moral decision – either leave the injured animal on the pathway and move on (that means having another go) or help the injured animal by taking it to the vet's and returning to the start of the game.

Continue playing, inviting the children to take turns to throw the dice. As they play, ask the children questions about their decisions. Would they want to be the winner if it meant leaving injured animals on the pathway? What is more important, being a winner or being helpful?

Discussion
Talk to the children about being kind and caring to all creatures, big and small.

> **Follow-up activity**
> ● Invite the children to help set up a vet's surgery in the role-play area using an assortment of toy animals, dressing-up clothes, bandages, boxes, pretend medicine and animal posters.

Differentiation
Encourage younger children to explain their decisions as they play the game. Explore the word 'conscience' with older children.

STEPPING STONE
Show care and concern for others, for living things and the environment.

EARLY LEARNING GOAL
Understand what is right, what is wrong and why. (PSED)

ASSESSMENT
Do the children understand what is right, what is wrong and why?

ON THE CD-ROM
● Photograph of a vet

Keeping us safe

This chapter encourages children to remember all the people who help keep us safe or rescue us in a crisis such as the emergency services, lifeguards, lifeboats and roadside rescue.

themes for early years

The police

Role play

What you need
Low-level tables; chairs; toy telephone; toy mobile phones; torch; walkie-talkies; dressing-up clothes such as police helmets, jackets, tabards and badges; note paper; small note books; pencils; tape recorder.

Preparation
If possible arrange a visit to a police station or invite the local police liaison officer in to your setting to talk to the children.

What to do
Stimulate some imaginative play by involving the children in setting-up a police station in the role-play area. Ask them to help decide where the furniture should be placed, where the officer on duty should stand and where to put equipment such as the telephone, tape recorder and uniforms. Include pens and paper so that the children can write pretend notes, messages, names, dates and appointments.

Talk with the children about their favourite police characters in storybooks and television programmes. Invite the children to take turns to act out roles and characters from favourite stories in the role-play police station, or use it for spontaneous play.

Discussion
Discuss how the police could help people in difficult situations, for example, a lost child, someone being burgled or in a traffic accident.

Follow-up activities
● Show the children pictures of police wearing different uniforms. Talk about the reason for wearing each outfit, for example, flat hats for driving, fluorescent jackets for safety.
● Show the children pictures of police who work in other countries. Encourage them to compare the different styles and colours of the uniforms by talking about the similarities and differences.

Differentiation
Help younger or less able children to gain confidence by encouraging them to join in role play situations with older children. Challenge older or more able children to act out short plays in front of a friendly audience such as peers, staff, visitors or parents.

Maths

themes for early years

STEPPING STONE
Recognise numerals
1 to 5, then 1 to 9.

EARLY LEARNING GOAL
Recognise numerals
1 to 9. (MD)

ASSESSMENT
Are the children
beginning to recognise
numerals 1 to 9?

The emergency services

What you need
Photographs, posters or toy models of a fire engine, police car and ambulance; felt-tipped pens; pencils; scissors; long display board at the children's own height; photocopiable page 45, '999'; on-screen activity 'Emergency service vehicles' on the CD-ROM.

What to do
Encourage the children to complete the on-screen jigsaw activity 'Emergency service vehicles' and talk about the types of vehicles that might come if the emergency services were called. Show the children photographs, posters or toy models of a fire engine, police car and ambulance and ask them to name and identify the different vehicles.

Provide the children with a copy of photocopiable page 45, '999'. Help them to identify the numbers one to nine and then to follow the numbers on the main picture in the correct order to reveal an emergency service vehicle. Once they have completed the main vehicle, encourage them to try the smaller dot-to-dot pictures. What shapes can they see?

Invite the children to decorate the picture and to cut it out. Help the children to create a simple counting display by glueing nine emergency service vehicle pictures in a row and labelling them one to nine. Ask the children to draw one to nine smiley faces next to each picture to represent the number of people helped by each vehicle.

Discussion
Talk to the children about the important role of the emergency services. Ask questions such as: *What number should you ring for the emergency services? Which services will they offer? Why might someone need the emergency services?*

Follow-up activities
- Help the children to draw or paint a simple road plan on large sheet of card. Include a car park and several roads that are wide, narrow, winding and straight. Provide toy vehicles, including emergency service models, for the children to count and park.
- Encourage the children to use construction bricks to create a simple model of a hospital, fire station or police station to stand on the road plan.
- Say the poem 'The firemen' on page 87 or listen to it on the CD-ROM and talk about the physical effort involved in working for the emergency services.
- Sing 'Whose hat is that?' on page 84 together.

Differentiation
Help younger or less able children to follow the numbers on the dot-to-dot picture in the correct order. Encourage older or more able children to assemble a counting display showing numbers up to 15.

ON THE CD-ROM
- Photocopiable sheet '999'
- On-screen activity 'Emergency service vehicles'
- Poem 'The firemen'
- Song 'Whose hat is that?'

999

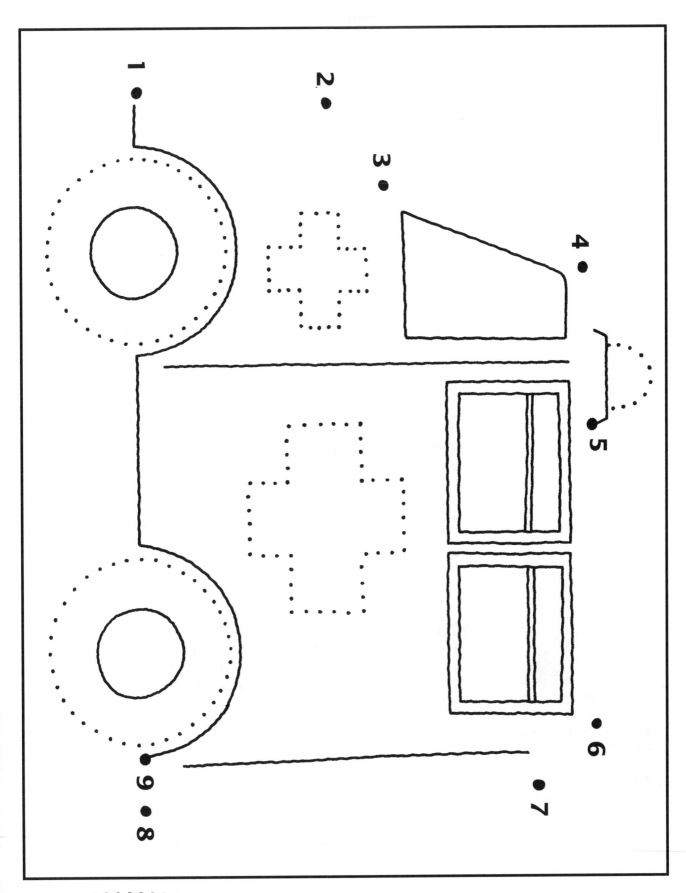

Sound

themes for early years

Firefighters

STEPPING STONE
Respond to sound with body movement.

EARLY LEARNING GOAL
Recognise and explore how sounds can be changed, sing simple songs from memory, recognise repeated sounds and sound patterns and match movements to music. (CD)

ASSESSMENT
Do the children enjoy exploring how sounds can be created and changed? Are they beginning to sing simple songs from memory?

What you need
Children's stories about firefighters; percussion instruments such as triangle, bells, scrapers, drums and tambourines; felt-tipped pens; pencils; photocopiable page 47, 'The rescue'; poem 'The fire appliance is here' on page 87 or on the CD-ROM; film clip of firefighters.

What to do
Read stories about firefighters to the children and talk about the ways in which firefighters help us. Can anybody recreate the sound of the siren that comes from the fire engine when it is rushing to the scene of a fire? Give the children a variety of percussion instruments and invite them to have a go at making repeated sounds to represent a siren.

When the children are happy with their siren sounds, encourage them to repeat the sound while saying the poem, 'The fire appliance is here' on page 87. When you have said the poem a few times, give each child a copy of photocopiable page 47, 'The rescue'. Talk about the pictures and then invite the children to cut them out and place them in the correct order.

Talk about the sequence of events that are happening in the pictures. Encourage the children to think about what might have happened before and after these pictures.

Discussion
Observe and talk about the film clip of firefighters with the children.

Follow-up activities
● Glue the pictures from the photocopiable sheet into a book and help the children to write captions underneath to explain the sequence of events.
● Create a number game display based on *Snakes and ladders* see page 76.
● Share the poem 'One firefighter, two firefighters' and the poem 'The fireman' both on page 87 and sing the song 'Whose hat is that?' on page 84.

Differentiation
Provide younger or less able children with one enlarged copy of the photocopiable sheet for a group of children to share. Encourage older or more able children to draw a picture showing what might have happened before or after the event.

ON THE CD-ROM
● Film clip of firefighters
● Poem 'One firefighter, two firefighters'
● Poem 'The fire appliance is here'
● Poem 'The fireman'
● Song 'Whose hat is that?'
● Photocopiable sheet 'The rescue'

The rescue

The lifeboat crew

What you need
Photocopiable page 49, 'Out at sea'; scissors; paints or coloured pens and pencils; card (approximately 25cm by 50cm and A4); hole-punch; string or wool; pictures, photographs or information books about lifeboats; sticky tape.

What to do
Give each child a copy of photocopiable page 49, 'Out at sea' copied onto card and invite them to colour in and cut out the picture. Help them to punch two holes in both ends of the lifeboat picture and to thread a 50cm length of string through the two upper holes and a second length of string, through the two lower holes. Put to one side for use later (see illustration).

Next, provide each child with a long strip of card and invite them to decorate it with a simple sun, sea and sky scene using paints, felt-tipped pens or crayons. When dry, ask the children to draw or paint a simple silhouette of someone stranded in the water and to punch two holes in either end of the sea scene.

Invite the children to place the lifeboat on the sea and to thread the loose ends of string on the left-hand side of the boat through the two left-hand holes in the sea scene. Tape the loose ends at the back of the sea scene. Repeat on the other side so that both lengths of string are pulled taut across the front of the sea (see illustration).

Show the children how to move the lifeboat back and forth across the sea, as if searching for the stranded swimmer.

Discussion
Encourage the children to use the moving picture to inspire imaginative stories about a sea rescue.

Follow-up activity
● Help a group of children to create an enlarged version of the moving picture using an A3 copy of the lifeboat. Provide collage materials for the sea scene.

Differentiation
Provide younger or less able children with hand-over-hand support. Encourage older or more able children to write or tape record a short story about the scene.

Out at sea

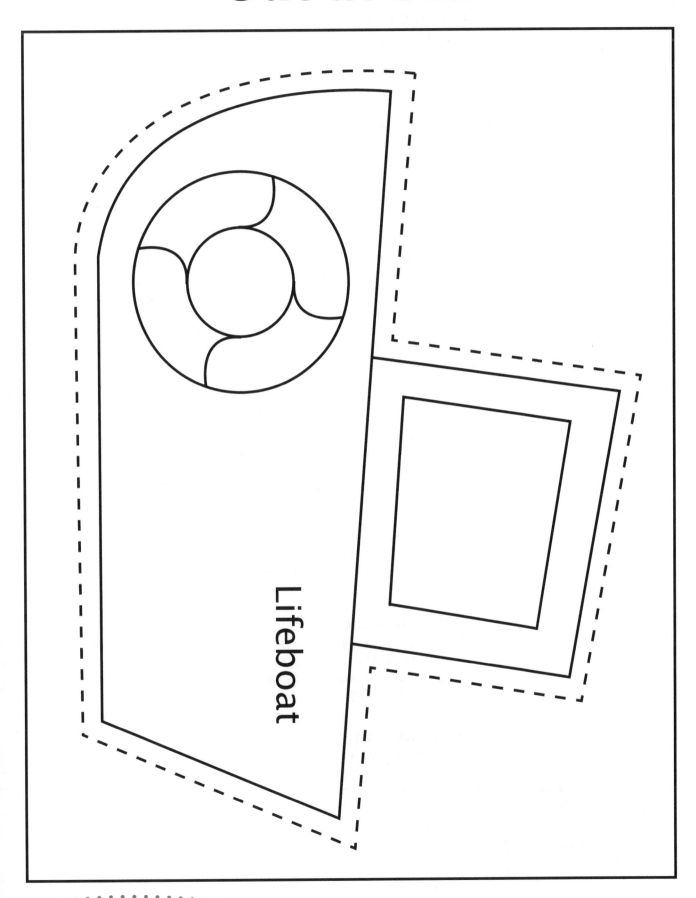

Lifeboat

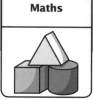

Maths

The lifeguard

What you need
A simple template of a T-shirt shape; three pens in different colours; large sheet of paper; photograph of a lifeguard from the CD-ROM.

Preparation
Draw around the T-shirt template six times on a large sheet of paper. Divide each shape into three sections. Photocopy one for each child or group of children.

What to do
Look at the photograph of the lifeguard and talk to the children about how they can help people at the swimming pool or on the beach. Talk about the type of clothes that would be suitable for a lifeguard to wear and discuss why lifeguards need to see and be seen clearly.

Invite the children to decorate some T-shirt shapes using bright colours to represent the highly visible outfits that lifeguards need to wear. Provide the children with three different coloured pens or pencils and a page of stripy T-shirt shapes. Challenge them to find out how many different colour combinations they can create by colouring each T-shirt in a different way using one or more of their three pens. Encourage the children to predict how many different combinations they could make. Will it be more or less than six?

Ask the children to describe the different patterns and sequences by listing the colour combinations on each T-shirt, for example, red, red, blue or blue, yellow, blue or red, blue, yellow. Challenge them further by drawing four more T-shirt shapes for them to decorate using the same three colours.

Encourage the children to explain the similarities and differences between the patterns on the six T-shirt shapes.

Discussion
If possible, take the children to a local swimming pool to talk to the lifeguards about their work. Alternatively ask a lifeguard to visit your setting

> ### Follow-up activities
> ● Provide fabric paints and sponges in different shapes and sizes and let the children decorate real T-shirts.
> ● Encourage the children to wear their decorated T-shirts for role play about lifeguards.

Differentiation
Provide younger or less able children with four T-shirt shapes to decorate using two colours. Encourage older or more able children to work out a sequence or regular pattern while colouring three of the T-shirt shapes, for example (r=red, b=blue, g=green): rrg, rrb, rrr or ggr, ggb, ggg.

STEPPING STONE
Show curiosity and observation by talking about shapes, how they are the same or why some are different.

EARLY LEARNING GOAL
Use developing mathematical ideas and methods to solve practical problems. (MD)

ASSESSMENT
Do the children show an interest in shapes and patterns by asking questions or making observations as they work?

ON THE CD-ROM
● Photograph of a lifeguard

People who help us

Small-world play

Roadside rescue

STEPPING STONE
Use available resources to create props to support role play.

EARLY LEARNING GOAL
Use their imagination in art and design, music, dance, imaginative and role play and stories. (CD)

ASSESSMENT
Do the children use their model with other small-world toys to support their play?

What you need
Pictures or books about roadside rescue services and trucks, including the photograph from the CD-ROM; two cardboard boxes; strong scissors (adult use); paints; paintbrushes; light blue paper; black paper; scissors (child use); glue; thick marker pen; string; small toy cars.

What to do
Talk to the children about the role of breakdown recovery workers. Ask: *Why might a driver need help from a car rescue service? Have you ever been in a car that has broken down? Have you seen cars being towed or transported by rescue trucks?* Show them the books about roadside rescue services and the photograph of a breakdown patrol.

Invite the children to make a simple 3D model of a rescue truck using two cardboard boxes – one for cab and the other for the trailer. Help the children to construct the cab by painting one box in a bright colour and decorating it with rectangles of blue paper for the cab windows and circles of black paper for the wheels. Encourage them to draw extra features such as windscreen wipers using a thick marker pen.

An adult should trim the top off the second box and cut a ramp in the back to represent a trailer (see illustration). Invite the children to paint it to match the cab and to add circles of black paper for the wheels, then help them link the cab and trailer together using wool or string.

Encourage the children to use the model by manoeuvring small toy cars on and off the truck to simulate roadside rescue operations.

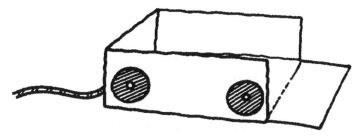

Discussion
Ask the children to discuss imaginary rescue operations or real experiences as they join in imaginative play with their peers.

Follow-up activity
● Help the children to use a thick marker pen to draw a large parking bay on to a large sheet of paper. Invite them to drive the rescue truck to and from the parking bay during imaginative play.

Differentiation
Provide younger or less able children with practical help such as cutting the paper shapes. Encourage older or more able children to think of a logo to write on the sides of the truck.

ON THE CD-ROM
● Photograph of a breakdown patrol

themes for early years

Safe crossing

What you need
Large sheets of paper; thick coloured marker pens; thick card; scissors; strong tape; stapler (adult use); long cardboard tubes or an old broom stick; local crossing patrol person (if possible); photograph of a crossing patrol person from the CD-ROM; poem 'Crossing the road' on page 89 or on the CD-ROM.

Preparation
If possible, invite the local patrol person in to your setting to show the children their uniform and 'lollipop'. Alternatively, observe the photograph of a crossing patrol person on the CD-ROM.

What to do
Join in together saying the poem 'Crossing the road' on page 89 and talk to the children about how the local crossing patrol person helps the children and parents who live nearby.

Provide large sheets of paper and thick marker pens and invite the children to draw a simple, bold design of a 'new' lollipop or crossing patrol sign. Encourage them to think about the best size, shape and colours to use for their lollipop or sign so that it can be easily seen and recognised by cars and children.

Ask questions: *Would a small or large sign be easiest for drivers to see? What would be more noticeable – dark or bright colours? Should your sign be tall or short, wide or narrow?*

Encourage the children to use thick card to construct a life-sized example of their lollipop by drawing, colouring and cutting out two signs showing the front and back view.

Help the children to attach the two signs, back-to-back, to the top of a long cardboard tube or broom stick using strong tape and a stapler. Invite the children to use their sign during role play outside.

Discussion
Take the children on a walk outside to observe and talk about other important signs and notices in the local environment.

> ### Follow-up activities
> ● Invite the crossing patrol person back to your setting to talk to the children about their models.
> ● Talk with the children about road safety or invite the local police liaison officer into your setting.

Differentiation
Encourage younger or less able children to work together to create a sign. Challenge older or more able children to think about a sign that could still be seen on a dull day by investigating colours that are most easily seen at night and by finding out about reflective materials.

STEPPING STONE
Begin to differentiate colours.

EARLY LEARNING GOAL
Explore colour, texture, shape, form and space in two or three dimensions. (CD)

ASSESSMENT
Can the children name, identify and differentiate colours?

ON THE CD-ROM
● Photograph of a crossing patrol person
● Poem 'Crossing the road'

Water

themes for early years

A brave rescue

What you need
Water tray; toy boats; long display board at the children's height; backing paper; white paper; photographs or art materials.

Preparation
Invite the children to play with boats and similar small-world toys in the water tray. Encourage them to create different water conditions to replicate calm sea and rough sea. Ask children to bring in photographs of their families from the past and present.

What to do
Read or tell the children the following story about a famous helper from the past.

> Grace Darling was the daughter of a lighthouse keeper. One day a steamboat was wrecked near to the lighthouse and many of the passengers were lost in the rough sea. A few survivors managed to cling to some rocks, so Grace and her father rowed out to rescue them even though it was very dangerous. Grace and her father were awarded a medal for gallantry and Grace became a national heroine.

Set up a simple time line and label it 'Now', 'Long ago' and 'Very long ago'. Ask the children to draw pictures about the story of Grace Darling to place in the 'Very long ago' section. In the 'Long ago' section, invite the children to draw pictures, or use the photographs they may have brought in, relating to past events in their own lives or the lives of their families. Repeat this with pictures of current events to mount in the 'Now' section.

Discussion
Use the timeline to initiate discussion about past and present.

Follow-up activities
● Turn the home corner into a lighthouse for imaginative play, using simple props such as a table and chair, a telescope made using a long cardboard tube and a cardboard box rowing boat.
● Tape a large sheet of fabric to the floor or table so that it is taut. Protect the surface under the fabric with a thick layer of newspaper. Help the children to paint a stormy sea scene on the fabric. When dry, hang the scene securely to create a dramatic backdrop in the role-play area.
● Sing the song 'People who helped us' on page 86 or listen to it on the CD-ROM.

Differentiation
Create a simplified, 'Then' and 'Now' timeline for younger children. Invite older children to add simple labels to the pictures in the timeline.

ON THE CD-ROM
● Song 'People who helped us'

Bringing us things

Children will encounter people who deliver goods and services in the world at large in this chapter including the postperson, farmers, fishermen and the supermarket delivery service.

themes for early years

STEPPING STONE
Talk about what is seen and what is happening.

EARLY LEARNING GOAL
Look closely at similarities, differences, patterns and change. (KUW)

ASSESSMENT
Can the children describe one or more changes that occur when making a milkshake?

ON THE CD-ROM
- Photocopiable sheet 'Internet order'
- Poem 'Shopping on the internet'

The delivery person

Food

What you need
Pictures of delivery people; milk; washed strawberries; bananas; mangoes; caster sugar; forks; plastic beakers with tight-fitting lids; straws with large holes; plastic bowls; hand-washing facilities.

Preparation
Check for food allergies or any dietary requirements before commencing this activity. Ask the children to wash their hands and put on an apron.

What to do
Show the children pictures of delivery people at work. Talk about the type of delivery people that visit the children's homes.

Invite the children to make some healthy milkshakes. Give each child some soft fruit such as three or four strawberries, a small banana or half a mango. Encourage them to mash the fruit in a small plastic bowl with a little caster sugar. Help the children to spoon their mixture into plastic beakers. Add milk, leaving plenty of space for the milkshake to froth up when shaken. Seal the lids firmly on to the beaker and encourage the children to shake their mixture up and down and from side to side. The fruit and milk need to be mixed thoroughly for the best results.

Remove the lids carefully and encourage the children to describe the change in appearance of the milk. Invite the children to place a straw into their beaker and to enjoy drinking their milkshake.

Discussion
Talk about people who help us by delivering other goods. Discuss the type of people who would find it very helpful to have goods delivered.

Follow-up activities
- Provide the children with a copy of photocopiable page 55, 'Internet order' to cut out and stick in the correct sequence.
- Share the song 'Shopping on the internet' on page 95.

Differentiation
Help younger or less able children to shake the fruit sufficiently. Encourage older children to experiment by mixing more than one fruit.

Internet order

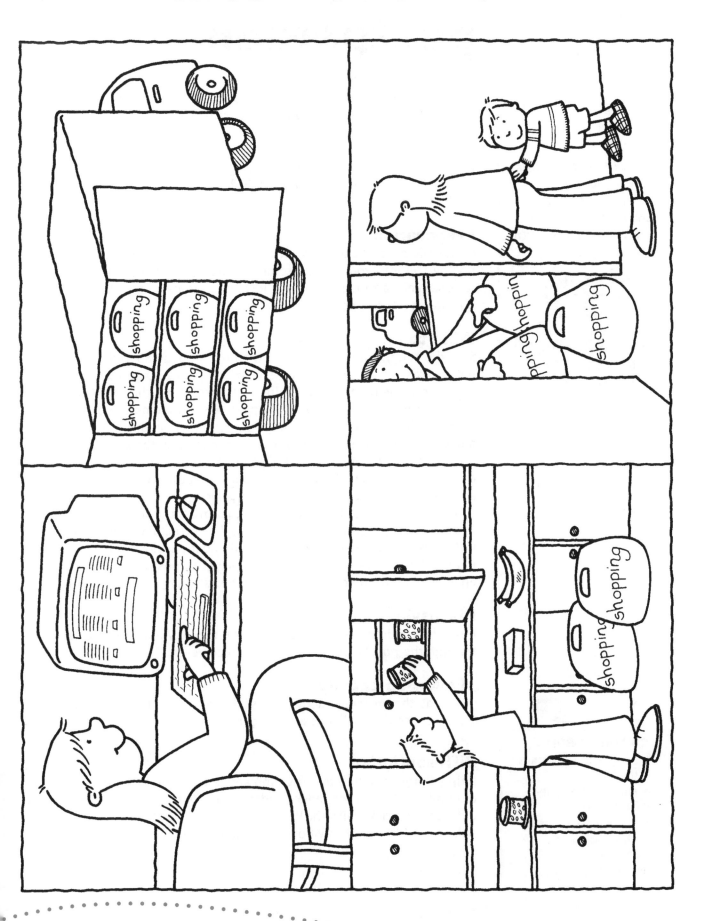

themes for early years

The postperson

What you need
Pictures of postpeople and post boxes, including the one on the CD-ROM; a postperson's bag (optional); a set of six small envelopes for each player (use a different colour for each set); a dice showing numbers one to six; strip of card (approximately 15cm by 60cm); coloured pens and pencils; song 'Put your letters in the box' on page 85 or on the CD-ROM; poems 'Postie, postie' and 'Guess who?' on pages 90 and 91 or on the CD-ROM.

Preparation
Divide the strip of card into six equal sections. If possible, invite a postperson into your setting to talk to the children about their work. Alternatively, arrange a visit to a local post office so the children can buy stamps or see behind the scenes.

What to do
Sing the song, 'Put your letters in the box' on page 85 and say the poems 'Postie, postie' and 'Guess who?' on pages 90 and 91. Look together at the photograph of the postperson from the CD-ROM and the other pictures and talk about how post boxes are emptied by them.

Invite the children to help make a posting game. Begin by drawing a door and windows in each of the six sections on the strip of card to represent a block of six flats. Help the children to label the six doors one to six and to label the six envelopes with the words 'Flat 1', 'Flat 2' and so on. Give each child a set of six envelopes.

Encourage two to four players to take turns to throw the dice and to post the appropriate envelope on to the correct flat. For example, if three is thrown then the player should post envelope three on to flat number 3. The winner is the first player to post all of their six envelopes on to the correct flats, or alternatively just play for fun.

Discussion
Have the children ever posted a letter? Have they received a letter through the post? If so, what did they receive?

Follow-up activity
● Play the on-screen activity 'Post the letters' with the children and discuss the challenges in the game.

Differentiation
Help younger children by providing a dice with one to six dots instead of numbers. Encourage older children to make two dice by labelling two old wooden bricks with the numbers 0, 0, 0, 1, 2, 3 and 1, 2, 3, 1, 2, 3. Ask the children to throw both dice and to add the score.

themes for early years

Parcel deliverers

STEPPING STONE
Extend vocabulary, especially by grouping and naming.

EARLY LEARNING GOAL
Extend their vocabulary, exploring the meanings and sounds of new words. (CLL)

ASSESSMENT
Are the children beginning to extend their vocabulary by seeking new words or phrases while describing familiar and unfamiliar objects?

What you need
Selection of small-world toys and objects that have different shapes, sizes, textures, weights and smells, such as a small teddy bear, book, soft ball, pencil and lavender bag; paper; boxes and other wrapping materials; sticky tape; string; poem 'Guess who?' on page 91 or on the CD-ROM.

Preparation
Wrap the objects so that the shape, size and feel of each object are not disguised.

What to do
Encourage the children to join in with the poem 'Guess who?' on page 91 or listen to it on the CD-ROM.

Show the children the mysterious parcels and ask them to talk about each package using words to describe their shape, size, feel, sound, smell and texture. Encourage them to guess and talk about what might be inside each parcel before opening it to see if they are correct.

Provide wrapping materials such as paper, boxes, bubble wrap, string, and sticky tape and invite the children to rewrap each parcel carefully so that it is disguised.

Develop the activity by asking the children to guess and talk about what might be inside the rewrapped, disguised parcels.

Discussion
Talk about parcel deliveries with the children. *Who delivers parcels? Why do people wrap parcels? What should be written on a parcel? What must be stuck on to a parcel before it is posted?*

Follow-up activities
- Encourage the children to use the wrapped and unwrapped objects during small-world play based on scenarios such as 'The lost parcel', 'The mysterious package' or 'Delivery dilemmas'.
- Read the story *Postman Pat and the Puzzle Parcels* by John Cunliffe (Little Hippo).
- Share books about posting such as *Harvey Hare: Postman Extraordinaire* by Bernadette Watts (North-South books); *Katie Morag Delivers the Mail* by Mairi Hedderwick (Red Fox) and *The Jolly Postman* by Janet and Allan Ahlberg (Puffin books).

Differentiation
Provide younger or less able children with hand-over-hand assistance as they rewrap the objects. Encourage older or more able children to help younger children during the guessing game.

ON THE CD-ROM
- Poem 'Guess who?'

themes for early years

The farmer

STEPPING STONE
Have a positive approach to new experiences.

EARLY LEARNING GOAL
Continue to be interested, excited and motivated to learn. (PSED)

ASSESSMENT
Do the children show interest and enthusiasm as they work and play?

What you need
Photocopiable page 59, 'The farmer's field'; felt-tipped pens; six small-world farm animals; two small-world farmers (or characters to represent farmers); a dice showing numbers one to six; access to a local farm or small holding (if possible); poem 'Farmer' on page 92 and on the CD-ROM.

Preparation
Try to organise a visit to a local farm, city farm, allotment or small holding so that the children can see what types of jobs need to be done on a daily basis.

What to do
Talk to the children about the many important jobs that a farmer does, such as sowing seeds, ploughing fields, caring for crops and rearing animals.

Make an enlarged copy of photocopiable page 59, 'The farmer's field' and invite two children to work together to colour it in. The game requires two players, represented by two small-world farmers. Encourage both players to place a small-world farmer anywhere on the pathway, then ask each player to choose one of the fields, in the centre of the two circles, to represent their farmland. Place six small-world animals randomly in six spaces on the pathway.

The aim of the game is for each farmer to 'find' and 'lead' as many animals as possible into their own field.

Ask the first player to throw the dice. If say, a two is thrown, then that player should move their farmer two spaces, in any direction, around the pathway. If they land on a space occupied by an animal they can move that animal, with their farmer, on each subsequent throw. When the farmer (and animal) land on the space showing the appropriate field gates, they can place the animal in the field.

Play continues in this way until all the animals are safely in fields. The winner is the player with the most animals in his or her field. Or just play for fun.

Discussion
Listen to the poem 'Farmer' on the CD-ROM, and page 92, and talk about the variety of jobs completed by the farmer in the poem.

Follow-up activities
● Help the children to glue a copy of the photocopiable sheet on to cardboard and cover it in transparent plastic film so that it can be stored and played again.
● Sing the song 'Whose hat is that?' on page 84.

Differentiation
Encourage younger or less able children to play the game with an adult. Older children can place up to ten toy animals on the pathway.

ON THE CD-ROM
● Photocopiable sheet 'The farmer's field'
● Poem 'Farmer'
● Song 'Whose hat is that?'

The farmer's field

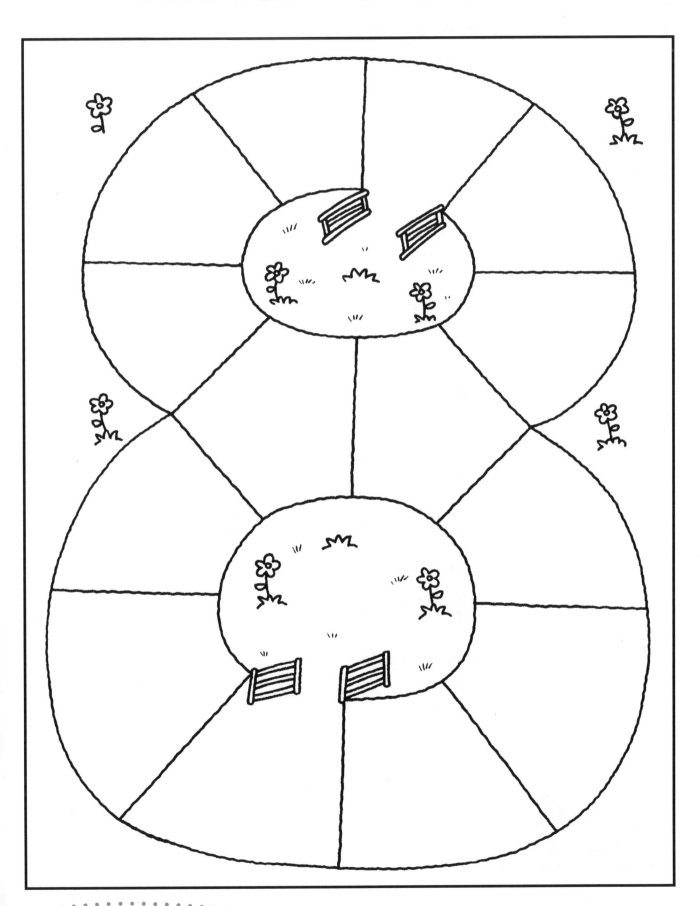

themes for early years

STEPPING STONE
Distinguish one sound from another.

EARLY LEARNING GOAL
Link sounds to letters, naming and sounding the letters of the alphabet. (CLL)

ASSESSMENT
Can the children identify the name and sound of one or more letters?

Fishermen

What you need
An alphabet poster or frieze; display board covered in blue backing paper; colourful card; scissors; felt-tipped pens; large plastic tub; Velcro; sticky tape; string; cardboard; fish-shaped template (approximately 10cm by 10cm); song 'A, b, c, d, e' on page 83 or on the CD-ROM.

Preparation
Use the fish-shaped template to draw 26 fish outlines on the display board. Label the fish with the letters of the alphabet and secure a small square of Velcro on to the tail of each fish.

What to do
Sing the song, 'A, b, c, d, e' on page 83 with the children. Place a poster showing the letters of the alphabet nearby as a visual aid.

Invite the children to cut out 26 fish shapes from coloured card using the fish shaped template as a guide. Help the children to label the fish with the letters of the alphabet. Secure a small square of Velcro to the back of each fish tail. Place the fish in a large plastic tub near to the display.

Cut out and tape a small cardboard hook on to a length of string. Secure the other end of the string to the top of the display board so that the hook dangles freely among the fish.

Encourage the children to take turns to select a card fish from the tub. Help them to say the name and sound of the letter on the fish and to attach it to the matching letter on the display board.

Continue until all the fish have been correctly positioned, and then remove the fish to play again.

Discussion
Initiate a discussion with the children about where different foods come from. Can anyone tell you where fish come from? Talk about the role of people who go out to sea regularly to catch fish for us to buy and eat.

> **Follow-up activity**
> ● Instead of letters on the fish, use blends such as 'ch', 'sh' and 'th'.

Differentiation
Display fewer fish shapes for younger children to identify, for example, 'a', 'e', 'i', 'o' and 'u'. Invite older children to think of a word beginning with each letter.

ON THE CD-ROM
● Song 'A, b, c, d, e'

Drivers

What you need
Four strips of coloured card or paper (approximately 20cm by 30cm); one sheet of card (approximately 30cm by 30cm); pictures of buses and trains and their drivers (include a variety of modern and old, real and fictional forms of transport); coloured pens and pencils; hole-punch; ribbon.

Preparation
Create a blank train book by securing four long strips of card or paper together using a hole-punch and ribbon. Invite the children to draw a picture of a steam train onto a long strip of card to use as a book cover.

What to do
Show the children some pictures of buses and trains and their drivers, noticing the differences between the different types of transport. Talk about how drivers help to transport people and goods all over the country, every day, and even throughout the night.

Ask the children to describe a memorable bus or train journey or to tell you their favourite transport story.

Show the children the blank train book and ask them to think of a name for the steam train, for example, Sam. Help the children to write the words, 'Sam the train chuffed' on the front cover.

Encourage the children to describe destinations and journeys for the train using words such as 'up', 'down', 'around', 'over', 'through', 'past'; 'hill', 'track', 'bridge', 'tunnel' and 'station'. For example, they could say 'up the hill', 'down the track', 'around the pond', 'over the bridge', 'through the tunnel', 'past the houses' and 'into the station'.

Help the children to write one sentence on each page in the train book to create a simple story, for example, 'Sam the train chuffed... up the hill, down the track' and so on.

Discussion
Invite the children to bring in favourite bus or train stories from home to share and discuss with their peers.

Follow-up activities
● Help the children to adapt the story slightly by writing about a modern train, for example, 'Sam the InterCity rushed up the hill, down the track...'.
● Sing the songs 'The driver of our school bus' on page 80 and 'We're all going on a bus tomorrow' on page 81 or listen to them on the CD-ROM.

Differentiation
Write the words for younger children. Invite older children to write the words using copy writing or emergent writing.

STEPPING STONE
Begin to be aware of the way stories are structured.

EARLY LEARNING GOAL
Explore and experiment with sounds, words and texts. (CLL)

ASSESSMENT
Are the children gaining an awareness of how to create a simple story?

ON THE CD-ROM
● Song 'We're all going on a bus tomorrow'
● Song 'The driver of our school bus'

Pilots

What you need
Books or pictures about pilots and different aircraft; ten sheets of A5 coloured card; coloured pens and pencils; thread; masking tape; cardboard; scissors (child use); sharp scissors (adult use); narrow strip of card; glue.

Preparation
Use cardboard to create a simple A5 template showing the basic shape of an aeroplane (see illustration).

What to do
Show the children the books or pictures showing pilots and aircraft. Talk about how pilots help us, for example, police helicopter pilots help to find lost people or track down criminals and flying doctors help sick people.

Provide the children with ten sheets of A5 coloured card. Invite them to draw around and cut out the shape of ten aeroplanes using the cardboard template as a guide. Encourage the children to decorate one side of each aeroplane using coloured pens and pencils.

Next, help them to fold the 'tail' of each aeroplane upwards and to write a number on each side. For example, the first plane should have a number one on each side of its tail, the second plane should have a number two on each side of its tail, and so on.

Help the children to glue the planes in numerical order along a narrow strip of card. Fold the strip of card in half, then attach a short length of thread to the middle of the folded card and two longer lengths of thread to the two outer edges.

Hang the three threads from the ceiling to create a counting mobile that shows ten aeroplanes 'taking off' and 'landing' (see illustration).

Discussion
Observe and discuss the dramatic film clip with the children. Ask questions to prompt thoughts and feelings about being saved and saving others. Would the children like to work in a profession that helps to save lives?

Follow-up activity
● Label the aeroplanes with one to ten dots, or the words 'one' to 'ten', instead of, or as well as, numerals.

Differentiation
Help younger or less able children to arrange the aeroplanes in the correct numerical order. Older or more able children could make their own aeroplane templates.

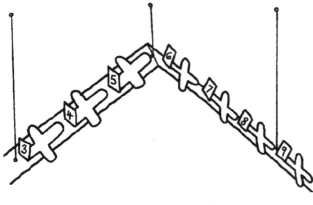

ON THE CD-ROM
● Film clip of a helicopter rescue

A sound invention

STEPPING STONE
Construct with a purpose in mind, using a variety of resources.

EARLY LEARNING GOAL
Build and construct with a wide range of objects, selecting appropriate resources, and adapting their work where necessary. (KUW)

ASSESSMENT
Do the children construct their models purposefully by selecting the appropriate tools and adapting their ideas as necessary?

What you need
Books and pictures showing different types of telephones; examples of real telephones and mobile phones (optional); toy telephones; a wide selection of resources for model-making, such as boxes, tubs, tubes, coloured paper, card, straws, pipe-cleaners, labels, string, cord and fabric; PVA glue; sticky tape; masking tape; felt-tipped pens; pencils; paints; paintbrushes; home corner or role-play area.

What to do
Talk with the children about Alexander Graham Bell. Explain that he has helped people all over the world with his invention of the telephone.

Show the children the pictures and real examples of telephones, then invite them to design and make a 'new' model of a telephone or mobile phone for imaginative play.

Provide a wide range of resources and encourage the children to construct their model using trial and error by adapting their design, materials or techniques as they work. Ask them to think about aspects of design such as the colour, size and shape of the telephone or mobile phone. Encourage the children to consider if and how to include details such as numerals, an aerial, a cable, a screen or a display panel.

When complete, encourage the children to use their models in the home corner or role-play area for imaginative plays and scenarios that involve using a telephone, for example, ringing 999 for the police, fire or ambulance service, or fantasy situations such as phoning home from another planet.

Discussion
Ask the children to think about the different ways in which the telephone helps us. For example, it enables us to contact the emergency services, to talk to family and friends, to order goods and to pass information to other people quickly and easily.

Follow-up activities
● Share the song 'People who helped us' on page 86 or listen to it on the CD-ROM.
● Encourage the children to construct other models, either familiar items or fantasy objects, to use for imaginative play.

Differentiation
Help younger or less able children with practical challenges such as applying glue, cutting sticky tape, writing number labels and trimming boxes. Encourage older or more able children to select and use the tools and resources with a high degree of independence.

ON THE CD-ROM
● Song 'People who helped us'

People and places

Help the children consider all the other people who help them as they explore the world around them with these activities. Including librarians, map makers and refuse collectors.

themes for early years

ON THE CD-ROM
● Song 'Pick your rubbish up'

The road sweep

Art and craft

What you need

Two large sheets of plain paper; paints; paintbrushes; small items of real rubbish that are suitable for the children to handle (for example, clean sweet wrappers, scraps of screwed-up tissue, torn labels, drinking straws); PVA glue; a photograph or poster of a road sweep; song 'Pick your rubbish up' on page 80 or on the CD-ROM.

What to do

Talk to the children about how road sweeps help us to live in a cleaner, safer and more pleasant environment. Show the children a photograph or poster of a road sweep and talk about the variety of tools that are required to do the job, for example, thick gloves for safety, a broom, a spade and a bin with wheels.

Provide the children with two large sheets of paper and encourage them to paint two identical street scenes. They could include a path, bench, grass verge, some flowers and a tree or building in both scenes. When dry, ask the children to glue scraps of real rubbish all over one of the scenes.

Encourage the children to compare the two pictures and to say which street they would prefer to live near and why.

Discussion

Sing the song 'Pick your rubbish up' on page 80 and talk about the importance of taking litter home or putting litter in the bin.

Follow-up activities
● Display the two contrasting street scenes next to a picture or photograph of a road sweep to help highlight the importance of a road sweep's job.
● Encourage the children to discuss how they can help to keep the grounds around your setting clean and tidy.

Differentiation

Draw a simple outline of two identical street scenes for younger children to paint. Encourage older children to consider why rubbish could be harmful to pets and wild animals.

Water

themes for early years

Window cleaners

What you need
Bucket; water facilities; cloth; windows within easy reach of the children; cotton reels; string; small toy bucket or plastic pot; coat peg or hook; aprons; photograph of a window cleaner.

What to do
Provide the children with a bucket and a damp cloth (or a bucket of water, an apron and a cloth) and invite them to help clean a low-level window. Talk about the things that a window cleaner uses to help him or her reach high windows safely, for example, ladders and lifts. Show the children the photograph of a window cleaner on the CD-ROM.

Explain to the children that pulley wheels are one way to help pull objects up or let objects down gently. On very large buildings, such as office blocks, window cleaners travel up to the highest windows in large cages that are moved up and down by pulley wheels. Some window cleaners also use pulleys to get supplies of water up to the tops of tall buildings.

Invite the children to construct a toy lift using a simple pulley wheel that they can use for imaginative play. For example, they could make a pulley wheel that will lift a toy bucket and cloth. Help the children to thread a piece of string through a cotton reel and tie it to form a loop (see illustration). Hang this over a hook, such as a coat peg. Tie a second piece of string to a small toy bucket, then drape the string tied to the bucket over the cotton reel (see illustration). Show the children how to pull the bucket up, then to lower it down gently.

Discussion
Explore and discuss what happens if the children pull the bucket up too fast, or let the string go suddenly.

Follow-up activities
- Invite the children to set up the pulley system outside to raise and lower small buckets of water.
- Encourage explorative play by providing the children with a water tray and equipment for pouring, filling and showering.

Differentiation
Help younger or less able children to thread, tie and knot the string. Encourage older children to test the pulley system by lifting and lowering objects of different weights, shapes and sizes.

ON THE CD-ROM
- Photograph of a window cleaner

Stories and rhymes

themes for early years

The librarian

What you need
Photocopiable page 67, 'The reading maze' copied on card; book corner or library within your setting; a selection of fiction and non-fiction books; scissors; felt-tipped pens.

What to do
Talk about libraries and librarians with the children. Explain that librarians help people to find their chosen book in the library by using a special number system. They scan the books in and out when people borrow them, and file them away carefully and tidily when they are bought back.

Help the children to set up a simple 'reading maze' based on the system offered in many libraries during holiday periods. The aim of the 'reading maze' is to encourage an interest in fiction and non-fiction books and an eagerness to talk about books.

Make card copies of photocopiable page 67, 'A reading maze' for each child to cut out and keep. Help the children to write their name on their bookmark.

Encourage the children to select one book at a time to read or to look at with their parents and carers at home.

When a book is returned to your setting, provide an opportunity for the child to talk about the book. Invite the children to colour in or place a sticker on to one of the 'stepping stones' on their bookmark once a book has been returned and discussed.

Discussion
Encourage the children to discuss the books they read by recalling the stories, describing favourite scenes and characters and explaining why they liked or disliked the book.

Follow-up activity
● Organise an area where the children can select and display a variety of books on a common theme, for example, flowers, cars or animals. Encourage the children to renew the theme regularly.

Differentiation
Encourage parents and carers of younger or less able children to come in to your setting to help their child choose and return to books. Invite older or more able children to design and make their own 'Reading maze bookmark' for next term.

ON THE CD-ROM
● Photocopiable sheet 'The reading maze'

People who help us

The reading maze

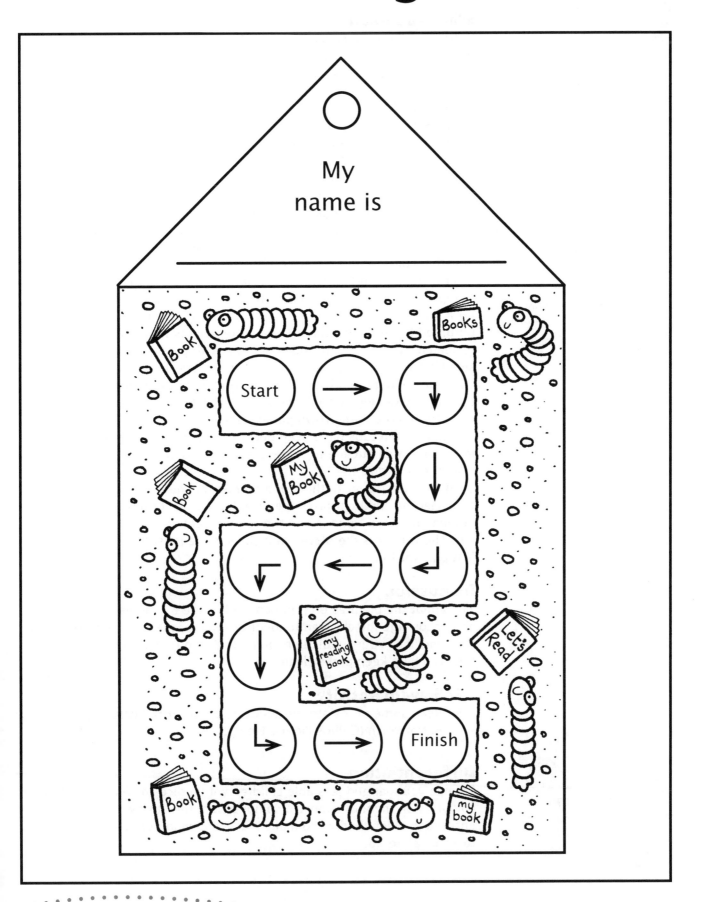

themes for early years

Park keepers

STEPPING STONE
Make three-dimensional structures.

EARLY LEARNING GOAL
Explore colour, texture, shape, form and space in two or three dimensions. (CD)

ASSESSMENT
Are the children willing to explore and experiment by creating 3D models and structures using a range of tools and materials?

What you need
Collage materials such as paper, card, crêpe paper, fabric and tissue; glue; ten large round ice-cream tubs; photocopiable page 69, 'Tools of the trade'; song 'Pick your rubbish up' on page 80 or on the CD-ROM.

Preparation
If possible, arrange a visit to a local park or garden so the children can observe the beautiful surroundings and have the opportunity to appreciate nature first-hand.

What to do
Talk about the types of jobs that a park keeper might need to do to maintain the area and keep it safe for people to enjoy. For example, they might dig out weeds, mow the grass, tidy away broken logs or branches, pick up litter, plant bulbs, sweep leaves and prune shrubs.

Provide the children with ten large, round ice-cream tubs to decorate to represent long grass, litter, bulbs, leaves and so on, as components for a floor game. To represent grass, the children could cover an upturned tub with green tissue paper or velvety fabric. Weeds can be recreated by covering the sides of a tub with paper leaf shapes and small balls of tissue paper to represent flowers. To make litter, the children could glue old, clean sweet wrappers or bits of newspaper to the tub. Broken logs or old tree stumps can be represented by covering an upturned tub with brown paper, tissue or crepe paper.

When all ten tubs have been decorated, ask the children to position in the play area outside to represent ten different jobs that the park keeper has to do.

Invite each player to think of a number between one and six. In turns, let the children throw the dice. If a player throws their chosen number, they can remove one tub to represent achieving one gardening job. The winner is the player who collects the most tubs. Alternatively, just play for fun.

Discussion
Talk about the pictures on photocopiable page 69, 'Tools of the trade' and encourage the children to identify some of the tasks and tools. Sing the song 'Pick your rubbish up' on page 80, to remind the children how they can help keep parks clean.

Follow-up activity
● Read some of the stories about *Percy the Park Keeper* by Nick Butterworth (Collins Picture Lions).

Differentiation
Provide younger and less able children with a dice showing six different colours. Ask them to choose a colour before they throw the dice. Encourage older children to make a dice showing numbers such as 11 to 16 or 21 to 26.

ON THE CD-ROM
● Photocopiable sheet 'Tools of the trade'
● Song 'Pick your rubbish up'

Tools of the trade

People who help us

themes for early years

Refuse collectors

STEPPING STONE
Show an interest in the world in which they live.

EARLY LEARNING GOAL
Observe, find out about and identify features in the place they live and the natural world. (KUW)

ASSESSMENT
Are the children gaining an interest, understanding and involvement in recycling?

What you need
Selection of objects that are commonly thrown away for example, a newspaper, an old item of clothing, a potato skin or apple core, plastic pots and tubs (cleaned); acrylic paints; colourful pictures from magazines; scissors; glue; varnish or PVA glue; songs 'Guess who?' and 'The wheelie bin song' both on page 82 or on the CD-ROM; poem 'The bin men' on page 94 or on the CD-ROM; film clip of the refuse collectors.

What to do
Sing the songs 'Guess who?' and 'The wheelie bin song' both on page 82 and say the poem 'The bin men' on page 94, or listen to them on the CD-ROM. Ask the children if they have seen refuse workers collecting and emptying bins and skips. If possible, let the children watch a refuse van visit your setting, or watch the film clip on the CD-ROM.

Talk to the children about the important job of the refuse collectors. Help them to list the variety of different things we throw away every week, for example, tins, boxes and food scraps. Discuss the reasons why we throw so many things away. For example, they could be dirty, empty, old or broken.

Show the children some objects that are commonly thrown away and ask them if they can think of ways to reuse them. Prompt with ideas such as recycling newspapers, taking old clothes to a charity shop and putting food scraps on a compost heap. Invite the children to find out about recycling from first-hand experience by making a flowerpot from an old plastic tub.

Ask the children to paint the sides of the tub with colourful acrylic paints. When the paint is dry, help the children to cut out pictures from magazines to glue on to the sides of the pot, decoupage style. Help the children to vanish over the decoupage to create a decorative flowerpot.

Discussion
Talk to the children about recycling and involve them in practical tasks such as collecting and storing reusable materials for model making, visiting the bottle bank, taking clothes to a charity shop or creating a compost heap in the grounds of your setting.

Follow-up activities
● Invite the children to plant a bulb, some flower seeds or mustard and cress seeds in their tub to take home.
● Encourage the children to help collect, sort and sell items for a jumble sale in your setting to raise money for a local charity.

Differentiation
Encourage younger and less able children to create a random decoupage design. Ask older or more able children to plan their design.

ON THE CD-ROM
● Song 'The wheelie bin song'
● Poem 'The bin men'
● Film clip of refuse collectors
● Song 'Guess who?'

themes for early years

Traffic wardens

STEPPING STONE
Operate equipment by means of pushing and pulling movements.

EARLY LEARNING GOAL
Use a range of small and large equipment. (PD)

ASSESSMENT
Are the children learning how to manoeuvre play equipment skilfully?

What you need
Toys with wheels, such as tricycles, scooters and pedal cars; an area outside with enough space for the children to move around freely and safely; chalk or masking tape; whistle; dressing-up items to represent a traffic warden (for example, a blue jacket or white shirt, reflective armbands, a hard hat); bold 'No parking' labels.

What to do
Talk to the children about the role of the traffic warden. Explain that they help to prevent accidents by making sure that drivers park safely and in the correct spaces. Encourage the children to join in a game that involves taking turns to be drivers and traffic wardens.

Use chalk or masking tape to create a 'car park' by marking out the outline of one parking space for each vehicle on the ground. Ask one child to dress up as the traffic warden and to place a 'No parking' sign in one of the spaces.

Encourage the drivers to move, in the same direction, around the car park. When the whistle is blown, the drivers should attempt to park their vehicle in one of the spaces. The driver who is left without a space is out.

Ask the rest of the drivers to continue moving around the car park, and invite the traffic warden to place a second 'No parking' sign, in another space.

Continue the game in this way until just one driver is left.

Discussion
Talk about the importance of fair play, listening to instructions and turn taking during games.

Follow-up activities
● Help the children to extend the game by giving the drivers a job to do en route, such as posting a letter in a pretend post box or delivering a parcel to a waiting shopkeeper.
● Invite the children to play a similar game using toy cars, a road mat and small 'No parking' labels.
● Join in singing the song, 'The driver of our school bus' on page 80 or listen to it on the CD-ROM.

Differentiation
Invite younger or less able children to play the game in small groups. Encourage older or more able children to think about why some spaces are labelled 'No parking'. For example, the space might be needed for an ambulance, it might be in a dangerous position or it might be needed by a bus.

ON THE CD-ROM
● Song 'The driver of our school bus'

Sand

themes for early years

STEPPING STONE
Describe a simple journey.

EARLY LEARNING GOAL
Use everyday words to describe position. (MD)

ASSESSMENT
Are the children able to describe a simple journey or a simple route around their map?

Map makers

What you need
A sand tray; small-world props and vehicles; a selection of maps; strips of paper in a selection of different colours to represent roads, paths and rivers; fabric in varying shades of green and brown; small boxes or construction blocks; a large sheet of paper; pens and pencils.

What to do
Talk to the children about the people who help us by creating maps and plans. Why do we need maps? Show the children a selection of maps, including one of your local area and perhaps a plan of your setting.

Invite the children to create a pretend town in the sand tray using strips of card for the roads and small-world toys for the props. Provide fabric in various shades of green and brown to represent parks, hills, and muddy fields and help the children to make simple model houses, garages, churches and schools using small cardboard boxes or construction bricks.

Help the children draw a simple map of the sand-tray town by copying the layout of the roads, fields and buildings onto a large sheet of paper. Encourage one child (or team of children) to describe a simple journey around the map. Invite a second child (or team) to follow the same route, in the sand tray, using a small-world vehicle or character.

Discussion
Ask the children to list groups of people who might find a map very helpful, for example, ramblers, drivers, ambulance crew and taxi drivers who are learning their routes or people visiting friends in new places.

Follow-up activities
● Collect other maps for the children to observe for example, copies of old or ancient maps, aerial photographs and imaginary maps such as the Hundred Acre Wood shown on the inside cover of most *Winnie-the-Pooh* books (by AA Milne, Egmont).
● Invite the children to draw a range of different buildings, parks and scenery on an enlarged version of photocopiable page 73, 'Around the map' to create an imaginary map. Encourage the children to use directional words such as 'left', 'right' and 'straight ahead' as they manoeuvre small-world toys around the scene.

Differentiation
Help younger children create a simple town and map using a single road, for example, a 'high street'. Encourage the children to describe the position of different features along the road using everyday words such as 'next to', 'opposite' and 'in front'. Invite older or more able children to design a more detailed town and map using straight and curved roads and pathways.

ON THE CD-ROM
● Photocopiable sheet 'Around the map'

Around the map

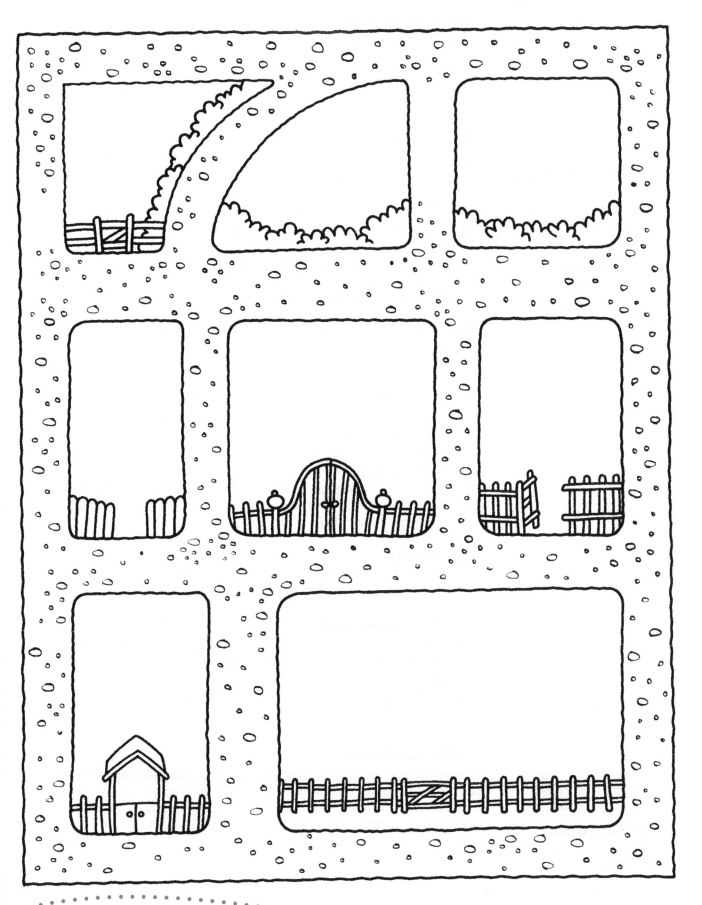

People who help us

themes for early years

A famous carer

What you need
Thick paper or card; blunt pencils; samples of real Braille (contact www.rnib.org.uk, The Royal National Institute for the Blind).

What to do
Read or tell the children the following story to help them understand how the actions of Louis Braille have helped people to this very day:

Louis Braille was born nearly 200 years ago. When he was only three-years-old he lost his sight following an accident, but gradually he learned how to find his way around by touch. Louis was desperate to learn how to read and write and when he was ten-years-old he attended a school for the blind. Louis eventually became a teacher and devised a special system of reading, called 'Braille'. Reading Braille involves feeling a pattern of embossed dots. Two years after Louis died, his Braille system was used in all schools for the blind in his home country of France. Today visually impaired children and adults all over the world use it.

Encourage the children to look carefully at an example of Braille then, with their eyes shut, feeling the dots with their fingertips.

Provide the children with a small sheet of thick paper and a blunt pencil. Help them to recreate the Braille effect by pressing the pencil gently into the paper to create a set of dots, for example, a line, circle or cross. Turn the paper over and ask the children to close their eyes and to feel the dots created by their peers. Can they tell which pattern of dots forms a line, circle or cross?

Discussion
Encourage the children to invite their parents and carers in to your setting to look, feel and talk about the Braille style samples.

Follow-up activities
● Ask the children to learn one of the Braille letters by touch only, for example, the pattern of dots to match the initial letter of their name.
● Share the song 'People who helped us' on page 86 or listen to it on the CD-ROM.

Differentiation
Challenge younger or less able children to create a simple pattern or picture using embossed dots, for example, zigzags, a smiley face or snowflakes. Challenge older or more able children to create an intricate design using embossed dots, for example, a spiral, loops or flowers.

ON THE CD-ROM
● Song 'People who helped us'

Displays

Displays provide visual stimulus and can help promote enthusiasm for a topic. This chapter provides four display ideas linked to the theme of 'People who help us'.

Our helpers

DISCUSSION

Encourage discussion by inviting the children to talk about their special helpers and why they have chosen them. Talk about the different people the children have chosen and the parts they play in the children's lives.

What you need

Small low-level display table or display box for each child; selection of colourful drapes; small cardboard box with flaps for each child; paper or card; glue; coloured pens and pencils; white sticky labels; folded card.

What to do

Provide each child with a small box and invite them to decorate the flap or flaps to represent opening doors. Give each child a sheet of paper or card that will fit neatly inside the back of the box. Invite the children to draw or paint a picture of someone who helps them at home. Help the children to glue their picture inside the back wall of the box so that it is easily seen when the 'doors' are pulled or pushed open.

Help each child to write the words 'Who helps me at home?' on to a strip of paper. Glue the writing on the front of one of the 'doors'. Help the children to write the name of their helper on to a sticky label to place on the inside of the door.

Emphasise the importance of each model by displaying them individually and purposefully around your setting on small tables decorated with a colourful drape chosen by the child. Invite the children to write a special label for their display table using a strip of folded card, for example, 'By Anna' or 'Simret made this model'.

Use the displays to encourage reading skills by inviting the children to read the words outside and inside each model. Help the children to write 'Find and seek' labels, for example, *Can you find a helper who is wearing red? Can you find Jon's mummy? Can you find a helper called Peter?*

Up the ladder, down the hose

What you need

Poem 'One firefighter, two firefighters' on page 87; display area; large cardboard base or large box lid; ten to twelve squares each of red and orange paper or foil (approximately 5 to 10cm squared); narrow strips of black paper or felt; narrow strips of white paper or felt; blue tape or foil; white sticky labels; black pen; yellow discs of card (approximately 5cm in diameter); glue; a traditional version of the game *Snakes and ladders*; a dice.

What to do

Say the poem, 'One firefighter, two firefighters' on page 87 together and invite the children to help create a number game based on the theme of firefighters, using the traditional game of *Snakes and ladders* as a guide. Ask the children to look closely at the *Snakes and ladders* game board and help them to count the numbers (or a line of numbers) in the correct order.

Encourage the children to begin making their own game board by sticking approximately 20 squares of red and orange paper or foil in a checked pattern on to a cardboard base. Help them to write a number label to stick on to each square. Invite the children to glue narrow strips of black paper or felt on to the base to create the shape of two or three ladders to climb up. Next, help them to glue narrow strips of white paper or felt on to the board to represent curly hoses to slide down. Decorate one end of each hose with a twist of blue tape or foil to represent water drips.

Finally help the children to create simple counters by drawing or sticking a picture of a firefighter on to a disc of yellow card. Display the large game board with the counters and a dice in an accessible position for the children to play with as they wish.

Use the display to encourage counting skills beyond ten, to count in twos, or to count in odd and even numbers. Encourage the children to use addition and subtraction up to three by providing two dice numbered 0, 0, 0, 1, 2, 3 and 1, 2, 3, 1, 2, 3.

A shoe full of helpers!

DISCUSSION
Encourage observation by asking questions such as, *How many helpers can you see? What colour is the door? Can you see a word beginning with 'm'? What would it be like to live in a shoe with all of those children?* Encourage the children to share ideas about how they can help to keep your setting clean and tidy.

What you need
Poem 'There was an old woman' on page 92; blank tape; tape recorder; camera (if available); display board at the children's height; brown paper; white paper; felt-tipped pens or paints; scissors; glue.

What to do
Say the poem 'There was an old woman' on page 92 with the children and encourage them to join in as you practise the poem on different occasions. When the children are confident give them access to a tape recorder and a blank tape and help them to record the song either individually, in small groups or as a whole group.

Provide the children with some of the cleaning items mentioned in the poem – dusters, mops and brooms, and invite them to take photographs of one another doing something helpful, for example, dusting a table, mopping the floor and sweeping outside. (Seek parents' and carers' permission before taking photographs.) If you do not have a camera, encourage the children to draw or paint pictures.

Help the children to cut out a large shoe shape from brown paper, or to paint a large brown shoe on white paper and then cut it out. Display the photographs or paintings on the shoe shape to create a display based on the words in the poem. Alternatively, invite the children to cut around their own drawings and paintings and attach them to the shoe shape.

Add labels such as 'mop', 'broom' and 'dust' and use the display to encourage word recognition and also to inspire story-telling skills, inviting the children to make up role-play scenarios about the old woman and all her helpers.

Mark of appreciation!

What you need

Plain white ceramic tile for each child; acrylic paints; very fine paintbrushes; aprons; shiny backing paper.

What to do

Talk to the children about someone that helps at home. What does this person do for them? Ask them to close their eyes and picture someone special and invite them to create a 'thank you' gift for this person.

Give each child a plain white ceramic tile and invite them to decorate the tile, using acrylic paints, with a 'thank you' message or sign, for example, a heart, a smiley face, kisses or the words 'Thank you'.

When the paint is dry, invite the children to help create a special place to display their tiles. Cover a flat surface with shiny paper and ask the children to lay their tiles on to the shiny paper one at a time to form a tessellating pattern. Talk about the tessellating pattern and encourage them to recreate it using squares of card or paper.

Encourage the children to bring their special person in to your setting to see the tile that is dedicated to them. When the topic is over, let each child wrap up their tile and take it home to give as a gift.

Alternatively, use the tiles to make interesting gifts. Tape a loop of cord or string to the back of each tile and glue a simple message, calendar or notepad to the bottom edge.

DISCUSSION

Ask questions about the display such as, *How many tiles are painted with a heart? Which tile has a green edge? Can you find two tiles that have the words 'Thank you' on them?* Ask the children to consider why a heart, a flower, a kiss and a smiley face could all mean 'thank you'.

Friends and neighbours

When you're feel-ing sad or lone-ly, Have you got a friend to share? When you're an-gry or in trou-ble, Have you got a friend to care? When you've hurt your-self and cry-ing, is a friend-ly neigh-bour there?

Chorus

Friends and neigh-bours, we need them all the time, So I'll be your friend if you'll be a friend of mine.

2. When you need to talk to someone
Have you got a friend to share?
When you need a hug and cuddle
Have you got a friend to care?
When you need some help with something
Is a friendly neighbour there?

Chorus

3. When you want to tell a secret
Have you got a friend to share?
When you're bubbling with excitement
Have you got a friend to care?
When someone needs a helping hand
Are you that neighbour there?

Chorus

Carole Henderson Begg

The driver of our school bus

He's read-y wait-ing there out-side the ga - te. He's al-ways ear-ly and he's ne - ver la - te. We climb a-board and say "He - llo" ___, He asks us where we want to go ___. He takes good care of us ___ _____, the dri - ver of our school bus ___.

2. He's always cheerful as he drives along
He likes to whistle as we sing a song.
He always knows the way to go

He takes it steady, nice and slow.
He's never in a rush,
The driver of our school bus.

Debbie Campbell

Pick your rubbish up

(To the tune of 'The farmer's in his den'.)

Pick your ru - bbish up. Pick your ru - bbish up.
Put it in the near - est bin or take your ru - bbish home.
Pick your ru - bbish up. Pick your ru - bbish up.
Put in in the near - est bin or take your ru - bbish home.

Jenni Tavener

We're all going on a bus tomorrow

Jenni Tavener

The wheelie bin song

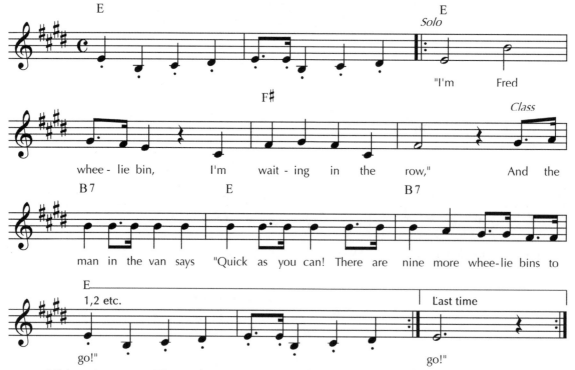

Have ten children in a row. They take turns to sing the solo tune, inventing a name for a wheelie bin each time. The class changes 'nine more wheelie bins' to eight, then seven and so on as each soloist sits down.

Ann Bryant

Guess who?

2. Guess who this is right behind the chair,
Right behind the chair,
Right behind the chair.
Washing, brushing, snipping at my hair.
Right behind the chair.
(Spoken) It's the hairdresser.

3. Guess who this is looking at my teeth,
Looking at my teeth,
Looking at my teeth.
Shines a light right in and underneath.
Looking at my teeth.
(Spoken) It's the dentist.

4. Guess who this is rattling down the street,
Rattling down the street,
Rattling down the street.

Takes the rubbish, makes the dustbin neat.
Rattling down the street.
(Spoken) It's the bin man.

5. Guess who this is checking all the food,
Checking all the food,
Checking all the food,
Bread and fruit and meat than can be stewed.
Checking all the food.
(Spoken) It's the cashier.

6. Guess who this is listening to my chest,
Listening to my chest,
Listening to my chest.
Checks my pulse and give my eyes a test.
Listening to my chest.
(Spoken) It's the doctor. *Hazel Hobbs*

A, b, c, d, e

(To the tune of: '1, 2, 3, 4, 5'.)

Jenni Tavener

Meet my dentist

Lazy Calypso

Meet my den-tist, what a nice man. He'll make you smile if an-y-one can.

O-pen wide, let's look in-side. Clean and white, well that's al-right.

David Moses

Whose hat is that?

Caller: Whose hat is that? Whose hat is that? Tell me please.

1.That's the hat of the far-mer, It's big and broad a-nd flat. There's

mud on the top and the brim goes flop.

Chorus That's how we know, that's how we know. That's how we know the hat.

2. That's the hat of the fireman
It's really yellow and fat
It shines like marge
And it's ever so large.

Chorus

3. That's the hat of the nurse
A small white cap is that
It's nice and neat
With a careful pleat.

Chorus

Music: Gillian Parker
Words: Trevor Millum

Put your letters in the box

(To the tune of 'Polly put the kettle on'.)

Jenni Tavener

People who helped us

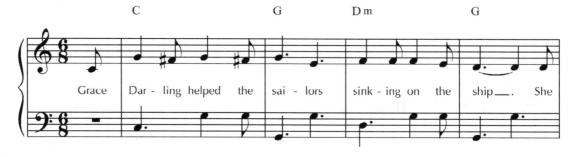

Grace Dar - ling helped the sai - lors sink - ing on the ship ___. She

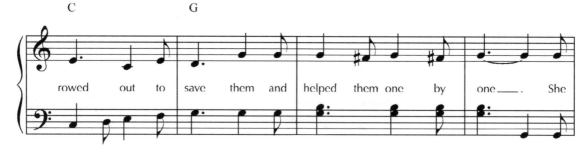

rowed out to save them and helped them one by one ___. She

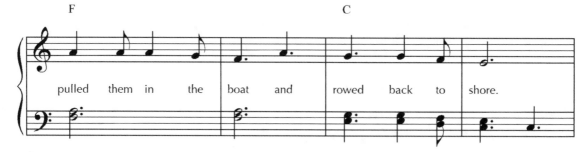

pulled them in the boat and rowed back to shore.

Grace helped save lives, we re - mem - ber her to - day.

2. Louis Braille was blind he couldn't read a book.
He made a special alphabet using lots of dots.
When blind people read, they read by feeling dots.
Louis helped the blind, we remember him today.

3. When Florence was a young lady, God told her to help.
She went to help the soldiers wounded in the war.
She cleaned and she nursed and she helped save people's lives.
Florence helped the sick, we remember her today.

Sally Scott

The fireman

Up jumps the fireman and slides down the pole
Runs to his clothes that are hanging on the wall
Pulls on his boots, puts his hat on his head
Drives away in the fire-engine, shiny red.

Down jumps the fireman and unrolls the hose
Turns on the tap so the water flows,
Sprays the building quickly, points the hose higher
Top to the bottom, right to left, puts out the fire.

Jillian Harker

Actions
Children seated. Bell or whistle signals the beginning of the rhyme.
Line 1: Children jump up, hold hands as if around a pole, go down into a crouched position.
Line 2: Run several steps, unhook clothes.
Line 3: Action of putting on boots and hat.
Line 4: Driving action.
Line 5: Jump down from cab. Move backwards, unrolling the hose.
Line 6: Both hands turn on the water tap.
Line 7: General spraying motion, then pointing the hose upwards.
Line 8: Movement of hose as in the last line, followed by mopping brow.

One firefighter, two firefighters

One firefighter,
Two firefighters,
Three firefighters,
Four!
Five firefighters,
Six firefighters,
Seven firefighters,
More!

Jenni Tavener

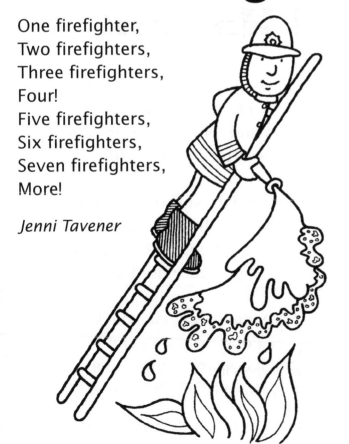

The fire appliance is here

The fire appliance is here.
It has a big, long hose.
The water sprays up very high,
And then it sprays down low.
Let's hold the hosepipe up,
Let's hold the hosepipe down,
Let's hold the hosepipe half way up,
So it's neither up nor down.

Jenni Tavener

The dentist

I love to visit my dentist
and read the comics there,
to see his rows of clackety teeth
and ride in his moving chair.

I love to visit my dentist
and stare at his stripy fish,
to see the pink fizz in the glass
and the fillings on the dish.

I love to visit my dentist
and see his tools all gleam,
but when I need a filling...
well, then I'm not so keen!

Judith Nicholls

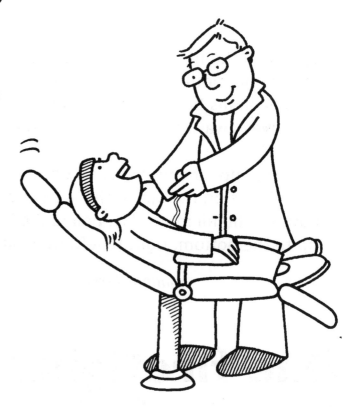

Haircut

Snip, snap, snickle-snackle,
just a *little* more!
Curls and twirls and tufty bits
scatter on the floor!

Snip, snap, snickle-snackle,
won't my friends all stare!
Dare I, dare I, DARE I look?
Is my head quite bare?

Snip, snap, snickle-snackle,
I don't think I dare!
Shall I, shan't I, open eyes?
Is there NOTHING there?

Judith Nicholls

Crossing the road

Cars! Buses!
Brrm! Brrm! Brrm!
Lorries! Vans!
Vrrm! Vrrm! Vrrm!

The Lollipop Lady
holds up her pole
and she makes the traffic STOP.
Then we all safely
cross the road
and run to the corner shop.

The Lollipop Lady
wears a big black hat
and her coat has stripes that glow.
When she walks slowly
to the kerb
she lets the traffic GO!

Cars! Buses!
Brrm! Brrm! Brrm!
Lorries! Vans!
Vrrm! Vrrm! Vrrm!

Wes Magee

Postie, postie

Postie, postie,
got the pip.
When my dog
gave him a nip.

Postie, postie,
in the snow.
How your ears
and nose do glow.

Postie, postie,
don't be late.
Bring my cards
...then shut the gate.

Postie, postie,
Valentine!
Mary Mousetrap
says she's mine!

Postie, postie,
at the door.
Pile of letters
on the floor.

Postie, postie,
ring the bell.
Wow! Big parcel
from Aunt Nell!

Postie, postie,
thank you for
bringing letters
to my door.

Wes Magee

Guess who?

Who's this coming
to your door?
Can you guess?
Are you sure?

Rustle, rustle.
What's that?
A letter landing
on the mat.
Who can that be?

Rattle, rattle.
Clink, clink.
Two fresh bottles
of milk to drink.
What can that be?

On the path –
sound of shoes.
Through the letterbox:
Daily News.
Who can that be?

Did you guess
(were you sure?)
who it was
at your front door?

Tony Mitton

Farmer

Before the cock crows,
before the sun shows,
the farmer is up and about.

She must feed the new lambs
and tie up the rams
and let Tibbles the farm cat out.

She sets about milking the cows
and then feeding the sows,
there's plenty of work to be done.

There's some feed to be mixed
the tractor needs to be fixed –
there's hardly a moment for fun.

The hen's eggs must be collected,
there's a barn to be erected
and it's now time to harvest the crops.

The sheepdog needs to be fed
before she goes off to bed,
work on the farm never stops.

John Rice

There was an old woman

There was an old woman
Who lived in a shoe;
She had so many helpers
She didn't know what to do.
She gave them some dusters
A mop and a some brooms;
Then watched with a smile
As they cleaned all the rooms.

Jenni Tavener

Here comes the caretaker

Here comes the caretaker
Sweeping with the broom
Sweep, sweep, sweep, sweep
Sweeping round the room

Here comes the gardener
Zooming round the grass
Zoom, zoom, zoom, zoom
Zooming very fast!

Here comes the postman
Darting to each door
Dart, dart, dart, dart
House, school, and store

Here come the dinner ladies
Serving up the lunch
And here come the children
Munch, munch, munch!

Brenda Williams

Actions
Move round the room with strong sweeping movements.

Race round, pretending to drive a sit-on mower.

Dart about pretending to post letters in different places.

Walk slowly, pretending to serve.
March forward, sit and mime eating.

I had a pair of glasses

I had a pair of glasses
They were pink and red,
I wore them everywhere I went
And even in my bed!
I lost my pair of glasses
But new ones I have seen,
I'll wear them everywhere I go
They're orange, black and green!

Jenni Tavener

Visiting the nurse

How are you feeling?
How are you today?

Stand on the scales
What do you weigh?

My! You are growing
Looking very tall!

Let me check your height
Stand near the wall

Let me see your hands
They look very clean

And I think your feet
Are the best I've seen!

Brenda Williams

Actions
Look interested.

Stand still and look down.

Look surprised.
Raise hand horizontally above head.

Stand up very tall.

Show hands.

Lift each foot in turn.

Use as an action rhyme or role play in pairs

The bin men

Crash and bang and wallop,
the men are here today,
to empty all our rubbish
and cart it all away.

They take it to the rubbish tip,
and there it has to stay,
and the busy, noisy dustman
come back another day.

It's dirty work for dustmen,
but they whistle and they shout,
and crash and bang and wallop,
so we know when they're about.

Jan Pollard

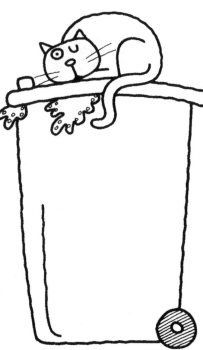

Shopping on the internet

Click, click,
with the mouse.
Computer shopping in our house

Click, click,
bacon, eggs.
Milk, bananas, chicken legs.

Click, click,
things to eat
Sausages and shredded wheat.

Click, click,
click on *Send*
Or the list will never end.

Click, click,
close it down
Groceries come from out of town

Click, click,
this is great
All we do is watch and wait.

Knock, knock,
on the door
Here's the lorry from the store.

Quick, quick,
open wide
Bring the shopping well inside!

Brenda Williams

Actions
*[Try to get a rap rhythm going
with click, click.]*

Tick off items on fingers.

Tick off items on fingers.

Point away.

Place hand under chin.

Mime knocking with one hand.

Click thumbs to fingers.
Mime opening door.

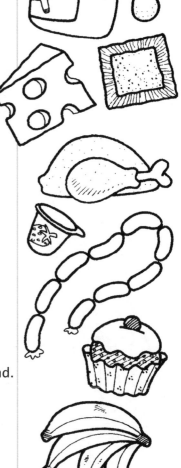
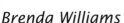

In this series:

ISBN 0-439-96559-4
ISBN 978-0439-96559-0

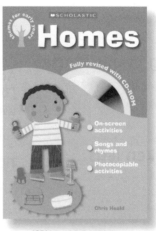

ISBN 0-439-96558-6
ISBN 978-0439-96558-3

ISBN 0-439-96560-8
ISBN 978-0439-96560-6

ISBN 0-439-96557-8
ISBN 978-0439-96557-6

ISBN 0-439-94497-X
ISBN 978-0439-94497-7

ISBN 0-439-94498-8
ISBN 978-0439-94498-4

To find out more about **Themes for Early Years** or to order additional copies
of the CD-ROMs call **0845 603 9091**

Visit our website **www.scholastic.co.uk**